the CASE for compulsory birth control

the CASE **for compulsory**

birth control

BY
EDGAR R.
CHASTEEN

PRENTICE-HALL, INC.
Englewood Cliffs, N. J.

To my

children, my students

and our world

The Case for Compulsory Birth Control by Edgar R. Chasteen

ISBN 0–13–115980–1
Library of Congress Catalog Card Number: 78–136308
Printed in the United States of America · *T*
Prentice-Hall International, Inc., London
Prentice-Hall of Australia, Pty. Ltd., Sydney
Prentice-Hall of Canada, Ltd., Toronto
Prentice-Hall of India Private Ltd., New Delhi
Prentice-Hall of Japan, Inc., Tokyo

Acknowledgments

To list only one person as author of a book is to exaggerate the truth. The fact is that hundreds of other people play a part: former teachers and fellow students, colleagues and critics, family and friends. To name them all would be impossible. To name none would be arrogant.

An earlier paper upon which this book is based was read and commented upon by a number of distinguished Americans across the country: anthropologists Margaret Mead of the New York Museum of Natural History and Ashley Montagu of Princeton, N.J.; biologists Garrett Hardin of the University of California at Santa Barbara and Paul Ehrlich of Stanford University; Ernst Mayr, Director of the Museum of Comparative Zoology at Harvard; demographer Kingsley Davis of the University of California at Berkeley; and attorney Johnson Montgomery of Redwood City, California. The Planned Parenthood staff and volunteers of Kansas City, Missouri, furnished me with information and valuable comments. Although not all of the above agree with my position, they all encouraged me to develop it for public debate and discussion.

Dean Bruce Thomson of William Jewell College, Liberty, Missouri, made it possible for me to secure the necessary research and secretarial assistance. Professor Earl Whaley, Chairman of the Sociology Department, cheerfully surrendered the departmental typewriter for the duration of this project. His constant encouragement and help can never be fully expressed or repaid.

My two student assistants, Marcia Calhoun and Barbara Stilley, worked long hours running down source material and typing the several rough drafts. Mrs. Faye Bateman, secretary to the Faculty, also assisted in the typing. Many other students performed volunteer and classroom assignments which contributed significantly to this book.

My wife typed several first drafts directly from my handwritten copy, a task somewhat comparable to deciphering an unknown alphabet.

The Institute for Community Studies in Kansas City, Missouri, granted me a leave of absence while the book was being written. Mrs. Lois Whitaker of ICS has been an invaluable secretary to me for several years, and she typed the final draft of the manuscript.

My children are too young yet to comprehend the problems with which this book deals. They know only that they missed countless games and stories because, "Daddy is writing a book." I hope their sacrifice serves a useful purpose.

A special word of thanks goes to Michael Hunter of Prentice-Hall, who, as editor for this book, performed brilliantly, making countless suggestions for strengthening it.

To the many not mentioned here, I can only say that the appreciation is no less felt for being unspoken.

To The Reader

I will argue that unless we act *now* to legislate a limit of two children per family, we have little hope of solving the other problems that beset us. You, the reader, are threatened. It is you who must take action based on the information in this book.

I have the credentials but not the personality of a scholar. For all the years of my graduate education, I was steeped in the virtues of objectivity, warned never to reach a conclusion before all the data were in and told always to allow the "facts" to speak for themselves. It was some years later before I learned that human problems have to be acted upon with the information at hand. The scholar's refusal to offer advice because "a study is in progress" or because "the data are capable of various interpretations," is an irresponsible act, no less dangerous than the deliberate distortion of public information by vested interests.

The twentieth century and its preoccupation with science has generated perhaps the most misleading half-truth ever visited upon mankind: "The facts speak for themselves." The truth of the matter is that facts are mute; they have only the voice of the one who uses them. Accordingly, facts are no more trustworthy than the intentions of the user. If you, the reader, are to evaluate the trustworthiness of what I have written in the following pages, then you must know something of my motivations.

I think of myself as a concerned and somewhat informed

human being. My concern is not for myself, for I have been singularly fortunate in acquiring a loving wife, three fine, healthy children and the only job I ever really wanted—that of a teacher. My personal ambition has been satisfied, but my public anxiety increases with each day's headlines. This anxiety has driven me to write this book, to present you with both information and a point of view which I hope will allow us to act more quickly and more intelligently on the most important social problem facing our country and our world—that of too many people.

Contents

	To the Reader	vii
	Prologue	1
1	People and Pollution	3
2	The Future as History	19
3	Overpopulation: America's Most Urgent Problem	23
4	Perspectives on Population Growth	51
5	The Mythology of Family Planners	73
6	Birth Control as Preventive Medicine	97
7	Barriers to Birth Control	125
8	Stone-Age Contraception	149
9	The Purpose of Sex	177
10	A Population Policy for America	191
	Chapter Notes	215

Prologue

In *Famine 1975!* the Paddocks draw a chilling parallel from military medicine. In time of war, the wounded are divided into three groups: (1) those who will die regardless of treatment; (2) those who will survive without treatment; and (3) those who can be saved only by prompt attention. When medical aid is limited, only the third group is treated. Applying this triage concept to the population problems of the nations of the world, the Paddocks classify India as "can't be saved." They also list 111 other nations which in 1965 received food from the United States under Public Law 480, and they suggest that many of them can't be saved.[1]

If that is true, and there is little to suggest it is not, then all the world is about to be engulfed by horrors beyond description. These doomed nations will not slip quietly into history. As their condition and its ultimate conclusion becomes clearer to them, they will lash out blindly and irrationally in a last desperate attempt to save themselves. Failing at this, their final act will be to ensure that other nations, particularly the rich and powerful ones, die with them.

1 People and Pollution

I define as most seriously overpopulated that nation whose people by virtue of their numbers and activities are most rapidly decreasing the ability of the land to support human life. With our large population, our affluence and our technological monstrosities the United States wins first place by a substantial margin.

—Dr. Wayne H. Davis, Biologist [2]

It's the rich—in a relative sense, the people less likely to starve—who wreck the environment. Rich people occupy much more space, consume more of the natural resources, disturb the ecology more, litter the landscape with bottles and paper, and pollute more land, air and water with chemical, thermal and radioactive waste.

—*Psychology Today*[3]

At the time of the first United States Census in 1790, Americans numbered just under four million, huddled, for the most part, along the Atlantic Seaboard from Maine to Georgia. Less than five percent of the population were living west of the Appalachian Mountains, and, with a few exceptions, settlement had reached inland only about 250 miles.[4] Living was hard, and only the strong survived. Disease, accidents, hard work and

Spartan living conditions held the average life expectancy of our ancestors below 40 years. Measles, diphtheria, whooping cough, scarlet fever, cholera, typhus, "consumption," croup, pneumonia—these were the killers of the first Americans. All but eliminated today, these contagions periodically swept unchecked over the country in the eighteenth and nineteenth centuries causing death rates of 45 to 50 per thousand.

This early American death rate is higher by far than that found anywhere in the world today. According to the 1969 World Population Data Sheet produced by the Population Reference Bureau, the highest death rate in the current world is 35 per thousand, found in several countries of Western Africa. Early Americans survived their high mortality rates only because of their still higher birth rates of 55 per thousand, higher than anywhere in today's world except for those same West African countries. Most of us remember hearing of Aunt Jennie or Grandma Jones who gave birth to eleven children, though only six ever reached adulthood.

But things have changed. The America of the 1790s has been replaced by the America of the 1970s. Only the name is the same!

The American economy since World War II has produced the highest standard of living ever known. We are approaching a Gross National Product of a trillion dollars annually, and if you are an average American, your family income is nearing $10,000 per year. You also work less and consume more every year. Some starry-eyed prognosticators envision the day when love of country will be measured by the amount of goods consumed.

We have all seen the bumper-sticker, "America! Love It—Or Leave It." Have you ever wondered how that "Love" could be measured? Well, Wall Street and the National Association of Manufacturers define the patriotic American as the one who buys, eats, travels, wears, uses, and destroys with the greatest abandon. They also salute the large family for producing more consumers.

Presently various levels of government from city to state to federal are enacting legislation and establishing agencies for consumer protection. And well they should! For Americans presently consume roughly 50 percent of the world's total supply of goods, yet we are only 6 percent of the world's people. We consume 12 times as much electricity, 50 times as much steel, 22 times as much coal, and 21 times as much oil as the rest of the world combined.[5] Our American standard of living is so high that only one-seventh of the world's present population could ever attain it.[6]

With the exception of some 10 to 30 million poor who are not able to express their love of country by using it up, the rest of us are credit-card-carrying members of AA—Affluent Americans. Those of us who belong to this version of AA experience delusion and hangover not unlike that of Alcoholics Anonymous. While on our binge we see visions of supersonic transports able to move entire communities in a single trip. We make death a preventable disease with organ transplants and "medical management." We grow food without land for people without number. We increase our leisure and happiness by multiplying our machines and factories.

But the morning after comes, and only the hangover remains. For Affluent Americans the morning miseries manifest themselves in the form of waste and pollution, and they do not disappear as the day progresses. Underfoot, overhead, and roundabout the by-products of our affluence assault us with their breath-taking, energy-sapping, beauty-destroying symbols of progress.

IN PURSUIT OF PROGRESS

Perhaps no other word so typifies the American spirit as does the word "progress." In its pursuit, the land was settled and made to yield ever larger supplies of food and fiber. Seeds and studs were constantly adapted to new environments in a successful effort to increase both quantity and quality of grains and fruits, fowl and cattle. The energy of nature itself was captured and put to work at the monotonous and tiring jobs previously performed by man.

With ingenuity and hard work, those Americans who preceded us were able to replace the horse with the internal-combustion engine. Earth-bound man was freed from his terrestrial prison by the pioneers of today's aerospace industry. The manufacturing process was made incalculably more proficient and profitable by the application of assembly line techniques and the construction of factories. Medical science practically eliminated contagious disease while achieving an average life expectancy of 70 years. Infant mortality plummeted downward as the chronic diseases of old age—arteriosclerosis, osteomyelitis, cardiovascular malfunction, arthritis, cancer, senility—replaced the former childhood scourges as death's vigilante committee.

In achieving our present long-lived, well-fed, underworked existence, we Americans took it for granted that Progress was a one-way street, getting ever wider and smoother with no toll collector to slow the journey. Bigger and better, fuller and faster, rang the voice of the profits, and in the name of Progress, America committed itself to the shortsighted plundering of its natural environment. Everything became a resource whose only value was in its use.

For example, the American mentality was well summed up in the question of a real estate speculator-turned tourist. After hearing the story of the Grand Canyon from a grizzled old guide and descending by burro into the Canyon's bowels, he turned to a companion to ask, "What good is it? No one can live here." Another tourist overheard, and berated the first for his ridiculous question: "Why would anyone want to live here? There's nothing to do, no golf course, no swimming pool, no hotel, nothing. What this place needs is someone with progressive ideas."

Progress has raped the land, and from this illicit union has sprung affluence—an illegitimate, though alluring progeny. Her measurements without equal, her customers without bound!

King-size, super-king-size, quick-sale, supermarket, best seller, come-on, fast buck, public relations—these are her bright and bubbly offspring. Unnoticed by the public and uncontrolled by her kin, big business and indebted government, affluence also spawned twin demons. Being hideous and small they were christened "waste" and "pollution" and quickly forgotten. But they are now of age and angry from years of neglect. Super pollution and gargantuan waste have laid siege to the affluent society.

America has given birth to a new species of pest not found in any zoology texts and immune to all the chemical warfare waged against more commonplace bugs. The litterbug prowls the countryside and the city street leaving its offensive waste to corrupt streams and woods, to offend the eye and foul the air.

Every year each American throws away eight times his weight in litter and trash.[7] Over a long holiday weekend alone, Americans throw enough litter on the streets, highways and parks to fill a line of garbage trucks 43 miles long. In a year's time the litterbugs excrete enough waste to cover a transcontinental highway a foot deep from San Francisco to New York City.

Missouri taxpayers paid $484,567.83 to pick up litter strewn along its roadsides in 1968. It costs every American from 30 to 60 cents for each piece of trash, each bottle or each can that someone has to pick up off the street. The cost of collecting and disposing of trash now runs to more than $3 billion a year, more than that spent for any public service other than roads and schools.

Economist Kenneth Boulding has called ours a "cowboy economy"—use it once and throw it away. Perhaps to say that we throw trash "away" implies that it is discarded where it is no problem to anyone or anything. However, in today's world, there is no "away." People, or at least the interests of people, are everywhere. One man's trash dump is another man's living space. An average community of 10,000 people disposes of approximately 1,000 tons of paper and 172 tons of metal each year from packaging material alone. And it's increasing!

As if the sheer volume of individual littering were not sufficient, the genius of American industry has marshalled its talents to produce waste products which are immune to the corrosive and degenerative processes of nature. *The New York Times Magazine* recently lamented: "Some things die hard, and to the embarrassment of a congested world their carcasses resist the acids of matter and of time. This is true especially of D.D.T. and the residue of chlorinated pesticides: it is true of beer cans and it is true of old automobiles." [8]

What a paradox that repair bills for American-made appliances and machinery are soaring due to poor quality and faulty engineering while at the same time mountains of indestructible waste litter our countryside and scar our cities.

The American business ethic has always sanctioned profit-taking above all else. In the value system of business, pollution and mutilation of the environment have always been legitimate if considered profitable. As business reckoned profit, they always were, for business counted only direct and immediate costs against which profits had to be measured. Thus, strip-mining, offshore oil wells, the internal-combustion engine, open-stacks, indiscriminate lumbering and hundreds of other shortsighted business techniques created great wealth for a few, affluence for the present, and disaster for the future. History may one day record that the apparent profitableness of American industry from 1875 to 1975 was simply the result of an erroneous calculation based on a mistaken assumption.

To Breathe or Not to Breathe

Have you taken a deep breath lately? In many parts of the country it could be dangerous. According to information published by the Federal government, the United States pollutes its air with 140,000,000 tons of aerial garbage per year. This dirty air shortens our lives and destroys our property. Emphysema, a lung disease directly related to pollution of the air, is responsible for 25,000 to 50,000 deaths annually.[9] Emphysema produces an anatomical change in the lungs which causes shortness of breath and a progressive breakdown of air sacs caused by chronic infection or irritation of bronchial tubes. It is the fastest growing disease in the United States, having increased 1,700 percent since 1950.[10] "In recent years, an average of more than 1,000 workers a month have been forced to retire prematurely because of emphysema." [11] Bronchitis, a disease which causes the lungs to produce an excessive amount of mucus and accompanied by a persistent cough, now affects one out of five of all American men between 40 and 60.[12] Lung cancer has increased rapidly in recent years and is twice as high in polluted areas. Air pollution is also a factor in heart disease. The heart has to work harder to compensate for the loss of oxygen in the blood due to impure air. The carbon dioxide content of air is up 10 percent and still rising. Pollution may also be related to premature aging. The dirty air of New York City killed more than 400 people in 1953, 1963 and 1966.[13]

Carbon monoxide and the unburned residues of gasoline belched into the air by automobiles drives oxygen out of our blood. Industrial pollutants in the form of sulphur and nitrogen oxides injure our eyes, noses and lungs. They impede our sunlight and limit our visibility. Hydrocarbons, the unburned residue of chemicals, produce cancer in animals and probably in people.

Each American breathes about 35 pounds of air per day, yet 60 percent of us live in areas government experts classify as air-polluted. According to *Science Digest,* physicians in 1962 reported 1,600,000 cases of illness in which air pollution figured, and the number is growing every year. Such diseases and health hazards as catarrh, tuberculosis, pneumonia, emphysema, dyspnea, headache, chest constriction, choking, nausea, sore throat and the common cold are all related to the impure air we are forced to breathe.[14]

United States chimneys belch 70,000 tons of sulphur dioxide every day. Ninety million automobiles pour 230,000 tons of carbon monoxide daily into our rapidly vanishing supply of fresh air. The Department of Air Pollution Control for the City of New York estimates the daily emission of pollutants from automobiles in that city alone to be 4,706 tons per day.[15]

Automobiles are presently responsible for 50 percent of all air pollution and despite recent pollution control devices for autos, we may be losing ground. Only new cars have the controls, and there is no guarantee they will be kept in operating condition. The reduction in individual auto pollution will very likely be offset by the increase in the number of cars.

The *Air Pollution Primer*, published in 1969 by the National Tuberculosis and Respiratory Disease Association passed this judgment: "Nature is fighting a losing battle with man-made air pollution; that much is clear. Vast expanses of countryside smolder and stink. Dreamy fogs are accomplices to murder. Sunny, windless days carry, like a disease, the threat of suffocation." [16]

Air pollution—the deadly lining of every cloud—is not confined to the East Coast nor to the big industrial centers. The National Wildlife Federation claims that air pollution is threatening public health, and not only in the large cities. The Federation's air quality index for the nation as a whole is rated "very bad." From Poughkeepsie to Pittsburgh to Phoenix, contaminated air sucks the life from millions of unsuspecting citizens. Los Angeles public schools restrict the activity of school children on days when the air currents do not carry the smog away. Mizzola, Montana, and Kansas City, Missouri, are afflicted with smog of sufficient frequency and severity to alarm their inhabitants. Asthmatics in Pasadena, California; Nashville, Tennessee; and New Orleans, Louisiana, suffer more than necessary because of polluted air.

As if that were not enough, air pollution does more than choke us all to death. It also eats away at the aesthetic and economic value of our homes and farms, monuments and museums, property and possessions. According to the *Air Pollution Primer*, "Cleopatra's Needle has suffered more in the time—less than 100 years—it has spent behind the Metropolitan Museum [in New York City] than it did in 3,000 years in the Egyptian desert." [17] *Today's Health* reported in 1966 that "the city of St. Louis estimated that land values depreciated $25 million per year for a decade before it started tackling its dirty air problems." [18]

Air pollution consultants say a family of four spends as much as $800 per year to undo the damage and clean the dirt left by air pollution.[19] The small city of Donora, Pennsylvania, lying in the Monongahela River Valley, saw the value of its real estate decline from 34 million dollars to 30.9 million in a year's time following a severe smog caused by industrial smoke.[20] In October 1948, an inversion of air trapped Donora's industrial wastes, sickening 6,000 out of its 14,000 inhabitants and killing 20.[21]

Today's Health reports that ozone, a chemical present in smog, "triples the rate at which your asphalt roof weathers away. Ozone also makes automobile sidewalls crack and also deteriorates rubber grommets, gaskets and insulation." [22] Other examples of property damage include discoloring and deteriorating paint, pitting and rusting metal, disfiguring limestone, shriveling shrubs and killing flowers.

Food costs are rising in part because air pollution kills off healthy crops. Cattle have died due to loss of appetite and stiffening of joints—all as a result of chemicals in the air which fell on the food they ate. The National Air Pollution Control Administration estimates agricultural losses due to dirty air at $500 million yearly.

After an excellent review of the dangers to health and property posed by polluted air, the *Air Pollution Primer* concludes by saying "the time for control is upon us." [23]

FROM SEA TO SHINING SEA

Do you think very often about your water supply? Chances are, you don't. But you'd better, or you'll find yourself saying with the Ancient Mariner, "Water, water everywhere; and not a drop to drink."

Lake Erie is dead, and the other Great Lakes are dying. Thousands of gallons of oil per day pour into the tributaries of Lake Michigan. Most of the lake's pollution comes from the industrial complex around its southern basin.[24] The Cuyahoga River acts as the municipal and industrial waste depository for the Cleveland, Ohio, area. So laden with waste is the river that it has been declared a fire hazard and has actually caught fire. H. G. Earl, writing in 1966, pointed up the growing seriousness of water pollution: "Across the vast expanse of America, the great river basin areas are getting their waters dirtied at such constantly accelerating rates, there is fear we shall run out of potable water, or, at least, in the next decade or two experience the dire risk of serious inadequacies of usable water." [25]

Cities across the country are now concerned that their water supplies are being made unusable. Municipalities are looking a little more critically at the expansion of industry which once they eagerly sought as the solution to their financial and employment problems. A number of cities have restricted the emission of industrial wastes, but most cities violate their own anti-pollution standards. Too many people, too much growth, and too little public money make hypocrites of our cities as they try to lead industries in paths they themselves have not trod.

Stewart Udall, Secretary of the Interior under Presidents Kennedy and Johnson, forsees the day when we may have to use untreated factory waste for drinking water.[26] A seven-fold increase in industrial water waste is expected by the year 2000. The National Academy of Science's 1966 report on "Waste Management and Control" estimated that the cost of cleaning up polluted water would run into tens of billions of dollars.

Air and water pollution is an increasingly sensitive issue in Congress and on campus. The President's Scientific Advisory Committee has a panel on the environment. The Federal Council of Science and Technology has set up a Committee on Environmental Quality. The National Academy of Science has an Environmental Studies Board. The American Association for the Advancement of Science has established a Committee on Environmental Alteration and a Commission on Population and Reproduction Control. The Clean Air Act of 1963, the Water Quality Act of 1965, the Air Quality Act of 1967, the creation of the Environmental Control Administration, all point up the tardy but growing concern of the federal government and the scientific community. Survival Day Parades, Environmental Teach-Ins, new environmental curricula and the popularity of ecology courses, student editorials and demonstrations, all give evidence that young people too, are concerned and committed.

In 1967 an oil tanker, the "Torrey Canyon," sank off the south coast of England, spilling thousands of gallons of petroleum into the ocean and killing tens of thousands of birds, untold numbers of fish and huge quantities of ocean vegetation. Beaches off England and France became quagmires of oily debris. Scientists of England's Plymouth Laboratories, in commenting on the disaster, spoke a fitting epitaph for the whole of America. "We are progressively making a slum of nature and may eventually find that we are enjoying the benefit of science and industry under conditions no civilized society should tolerate." [27]

THE SOUND OF SILENCE

There is another kind of pollution. It fills the air but causes no shortness of breath, no hacking cough, no runny eyes. Cities across the country are finding it an increasing nuisance. Unlike the gases which stalk us unannounced and often undetected, this variety of air pollution comes on like gangbusters.

Noise—senseless sound—assaults the ears, destroys hearing, numbs the brain, impairs eye movement and focus, upsets body coordination and equilibrium, interferes with rest and convalescence, prevents concentrated mental effort, causes stress and nervousness, creates tension, and contributes to cardiovascular diseases. Even family problems are more prevalent among those individuals subjected to prolonged periods of excessive noise. According to the World Health Organization, excessive noise costs Americans $4 billion a year in health expenses and lost pay. It is probably no surprise to you, but we Americans live in the noisiest environment ever to exist. We start going deaf at age 25 because of the constant din to which we are exposed. Many non-western agrarian people on the other hand can hear as well at 70 as at 20.[28] Noise levels have doubled since the mid-fifties and are now doubling every 10 years. *The New York Times Magazine* stated, "Well informed scientists reckon that if city noise continues to rise as it is presently rising, by one decibel a year, everyone will be stone deaf by the year 2000.[29] The Federal Council for Science and Technology called noise a major health hazard and recommended governmental guidelines to establish noise level standards.

Sound is measured in decibels. Named after Alexander Graham Bell, inventor of the telephone, decibels are logarithmic scale units which measure the loudness of sound perceived by the human ear. Human beings can tolerate sound of approximately 85 decibels without ill effect. Above this level, hearing loss quickly sets in. Temporary deafness can result from even short exposure to noise levels between 100 and 125 decibels. Permanent damage can result from any greater exposure.[30]

The transportation and construction industries are the chief noise makers of the United States economy. Studies have found high numbers of abnormal heartbeats in steel workers exposed to noise. Riveting, blasting, drilling, forging—all take their toll in loss of hearing and onset of disease.[31] Rock music groups attack their audiences with bursts of sound up to 120 decibels. Loss of hearing at high frequencies is becoming an American characteristic.

The kitchen is becoming almost as noisy as the factory. Mixers and blenders, dishwashers and garbage disposal units, separately and in combination, have more noise potential than the pneumatic hammer or the blast furnace. Customers equate noise with power, little realizing that they are committing prolonged and involuntary suicide. For health and aesthetic purposes it is recommended that the noise level of the individual home should not exceed 35 decibels during the day and 30 at night. This would be roughly equivalent to the sound level of a tropical beach.[32] But if you have been to a beach lately you know that even there such quietness is seldom found anymore.

As population size and density increases and more people employ more noise makers, the situation threatens to get completely out of hand. This realization has prompted local and national government to action. New York City in 1969 passed an ordinance to establish a 45-decibel standard for noise transference through walls of new apartments. In May 1969, a U.S. Labor Department health code set 90 decibels as the loudest continuous noise permitted for an industrial worker. If the level is higher, exposure time must be reduced. As the noise level of a beehive increases when the hive is enlarged, so American noise grows as American numbers expand.

POPULUTION

A new word—populution—has made its way into the English language as the relationship between population and pollution has become more obvious. The basic cause of pollution and waste is simple: too many people. In the first place, an increasing population necessitates the production of more goods. Most of these products are packaged in disposable containers which after only one use find their way into streams, highways, forests and sanitary land fills. To feed and clothe 100 people at the same level as the 50 previously living in the same area obviously requires twice as much food and clothing. "The larger the market, the greater the demand" has always been a fundamental operating assumption of American business. The other side of that coin is now visible though, and it reads "The larger the production, the greater the pollution."

It would be bad enough if the output of waste grew in direct proportion to the increase in the size of the population. But the consumption of goods and its corresponding output in trash and garbage in America actually outraces population growth. United States population increased by one percent in 1969 but the production of refuse grew by four percent.[33] The increasing level of affluence over the last two decades has transformed luxuries into necessities. The two-car family is a fairly recent but mushrooming phenomenon. Garbage disposals ease our overburdened dinner tables. Washers and dryers restore our miracle fabrics. Powerful detergents and enzyme-active presoaks fight our dirty battles. Per capita consumption of meat, electricity, gasoline, steel, and scores of other things has been increasing. It seems that the more there are of us, the more we all need and the more we all waste.

Thus does an increasing population have a two-fold impact upon its physical environment. It is like a businessman who has to increase the salary of all of his employees every time he hires someone new. If the employer has no control over the number of new employees, if he must, for some reason, hire all those who ask for a job, he will soon find his business in bankruptcy. Such is the imminent condition of our environment. Too many have taken too much, too fast, and for too long—it is now time to pay the piper.

Various levels of government are now recognizing and beginning to exercise their duty to protect the citizenry against environmental hazards. Air and water pollution, litter and ugliness have all come under the legislative gun. Laws have been passed giving local governments the authority to forbid auto travel when contaminants in the air reach a dangerous level, and Congress has established air and water quality standards.

"Every litter bit hurts" has become an often-heard phrase in American speech as we have begun to realize the staggering economic and aesthetic costs of the indiscriminate disposal of waste. Those who engage in littering are branded "litterbugs" and are subject to fine. Industries which contaminate our water and air are now being inveighed and legislated against by an impatient Congress. But it makes no sense at all to stigmatize and punish these offenders while allowing those basically responsible for all the problems to escape unscathed. It is not only senseless but futile to try to control pollution without restricting population growth. The first antipollution laws in America were passed in 1647 by the Massachusetts Bay Colony in an effort to prevent the pollution of Boston Harbor.[34] But we will never solve our environmental crisis by concentrating only on pollution prevention. The time has come to react to prolific parenthood as we act toward other types of environmental contaminants.

Dr. John H. Thomas, Stanford University biologist (and a Catholic), puts it bluntly: "There is an inevitable decrease in environmental quality as population goes up . . . *starting now,* it is immoral for any couple to have more than two children." [35]

A nationally syndicated columnist wrote in early 1970 that being against pollution was getting to be as politically popular as being for motherhood. While such a statement indicates growing concern with this ecological-environmental crisis, it distorts our understanding of its fundamental cause. For to be against pollution is to be against motherhood and fatherhood. Just as we are not permitted to dispose of our wastes at will, we cannot continue to create new people at will. For the creation soon becomes the pollution.

All efforts made to stop pollution will be overwhelmed by our pointless proliferation of people. But unlike the Old Woman in the Shoe, we *do* know what to do. We must quit adding people to an already overcrowded environment.

2 The Future as History

I think I know what is bothering the students. I think that what we are up against is a generation that is by no means sure that it has a future.

—George Wald [1]

The people of an era must either carry the burden of change assigned to their time or die under its weight in the wilderness.

—Harold Rosenberg[2]

The rise and fall of civilization, the ebb and flow of emotions, the birth and death of individuals—all seem to confirm the cyclical inevitability of human life. Geopolitics emphasizes the conservatism which overtakes a society grown physically old. The Youth Movement produces new morality and radical policies. We sometimes fall into the trap of thinking that human affairs are governed by a natural rhythm, inescapable and unresponsive: "History repeats itself" we are fond of saying, and having said, we leave our world to run itself. And for those who think that history repeats itself, it does. For it is only our willingness to submit that ever made it so. But I believe that people, not history, make countries and communities what they are.

A more accurate description of history's effect upon us is

given by the famous nineteenth-century German philosopher Georg Hegel: "What experience and history teach us is this—that people and governments never have learned anything from history, or acted on principles deduced from it."

Even this is not inevitable, however, flowing as it does more from our easily acquired tendencies toward stupidity than from any inherent and irreversible instincts.

If parts of history are repeated it is because we choose, either by deliberate action or unconscious inaction to have it so. If America makes the same mistakes as other civilizations before it, it is not history we should blame, but Americans. Written on the pyramids thousands of years ago was the cryptic message: "and no one was angry enough to speak out." History does not record the injustice which prompted this indictment, but it might have been any number of things which still plague us.

A ground swell of anger now rumbles across the United States. Directed toward problems of overpopulation and environmental deterioration, this babble of voices promises to halt the galloping grizzliness which grips our land and our people. But like all promises, it is as yet potential rather than performance. We cannot know until the future becomes the present whether ecology is a fad, of temporary fancy to the intellectual and the demonstrator, or an idea whose time has come. Depending upon our inclinations, we can find justification for either verdict in history. The *Silent Spring* has been shattered by *The Population Bomb*. Can Humpty-Dumpty be put together again?

Some years ago a brilliant satirist calling himself Professor J. Abner Peddiwell wrote a book in which he described *The Saber-Tooth Curriculum*. In the book, Professor Peddiwell tells how Paleolithic education came to center around three courses: fish-grabbing, woolly horse clubbing and saber-tooth-tiger scaring with fire. When originally established, this curriculum was intended to provide practical information to satisfy the immediate and daily needs of stone-age man. As time went by, however, people developed an attachment to these pillars of a liberal education, and when one day the waters were muddied so that fish-grabbing was impossible, the woolly horse had been replaced by antelopes and the saber-tooth-tigers had all been killed, the tribesmen refused to modify their educational content. To change their educational program, they reasoned, would deny to future generations the timeless essence of true education and would dishonor the memory of its founder.[3]

These Paleolithic men were victimized by the same erroneous reasoning which afflicts us. They could not see that things are done at a given time by a certain people simply because it needs to be done. To preserve the form or content of that action when the need no longer exists is to see the future as history and to ensure a more troublesome present than necessary.

So it is that our pro-natalist business ethics, our political and social support for the large family, our theologically buttressed breeding proclivities were all designed to satisfy a need for more people—a need which no longer exists. To retain these outdated philosophies and policies is to overlook or deny that our needs have changed. The need today is for fewer people rather than more. Present need rather than historical habit must be allowed to shape our future. Else there may be no future.

Another cliché often heard argues that "He who doesn't know history is destined to repeat it." In this I find a great deal of truth and some hope. If it does not provide us with better approaches to the problems of our day; if there are no principles to be extracted; if history is as dead as the particular personalities and events it describes, then history is no more relevant to our time than tiger-scaring and horse-clubbing.

But history makes two things crystal clear. In order to survive, the people of a society must involve themselves in its actions and decisions. If they do not, there will not be the necessary variety and alternatives essential for successful adaptation to novel conditions and changing needs. But involvement alone is not enough; it must be directed by information. We have to know what needs to be done and how it can be accomplished. If we don't, our involvement is likely to be spasmodic and misdirected, compounding rather than alleviating the problem. To be involved without being informed is dangerous. To be informed without being involved is sterile.

Americans usually attempt to solve a problem after it has reached the crisis stage. If history repeats, we will act to bring about compulsory birth control only after massive starvation, global wars, political chaos, personal destruction. The modern riding companions of the Four Horsemen of the Apocalypse will be loosed among us, and we will be in our customary position of shutting the barn door after the horse has escaped.

But if we can ask the right questions, recognize the important issues, pursue the most urgent causes, apply sufficient intelligence and determination—if we can do all these things we will escape the seeming inevitability of history. We can chart new paths rather than stumbling blindly down old ones simply because they are available.

Will some future historian write a ponderous tome called, *The Rise and Fall of American Civilization*? Or will we act while there is yet time to disengage ourselves from the quiet dogmas of the past? Do we have what it takes to assume the burden of change assigned to our age?

In an essay called "What Is the World's Greatest Need?" C. P. Snow says, "All healthy societies are ready to sacrifice the existential moment for their children's future and for children after these. The sense of the future is behind all good policies. Unless we have it, we can give nothing either wise or decent to the world." [4]

3 Overpopulation: America's Most Urgent Problem

Whatever your cause, it's a lost cause unless we control population.

—Hugh Moore Fund [1]

No one knows exactly how long man has lived on the earth. Most anthropologists date the first human life at about 500,000 years ago, while some push the date back to a million, a million and a half, and a few even suggest that man has roamed the planet for two million years. Nor are we sure in what part of the world human life first appeared. Until recently it was fairly well assumed that man had originated in Central Europe in the form of Neanderthal and Cro-Magnon. Evidence is now appearing, however, to suggest that East Africa may have been the cradle of mankind.

Whatever the date and place of man's beginning, it is certain that this planet of ours was without human life for much longer than it has been with it. The Earth is approximately four billion years old, which means that it has existed 2 to 4 thousand years for each year man has been on it.

Just as we do not know exactly when or where man originated, we cannot be absolutely certain about the rate of growth of the human population or its current size. Obviously there were no census takers calling on Neolithic man. Pre-historians, archeologists, anthropologists and demographers have carefully reconstructed all available data to arrive at estimates of early population size. For some medieval populations, however, more precise information is available. Following his invasion of England in 1066, William the Conqueror commanded a census of his new possession. Completed in 1086, the Domesday Book may be seen today in the Public Record Office of England.

Early man was a hunter and gatherer, incessantly foraging the countryside in search of food, living constantly on the brink of starvation. Biologist Marston Bates believes that "the maximum possible population for the whole world in the Old Stone Age would have been about 10 million." [2] For tens of thousands of years population size remained fairly constant. Then, about 8,000 B.C. an event occurred which radically altered man's relationship to the Earth: The Neolithic or Agricultural Revolution, we call it today. It is difficult for any of us, accustomed as we are to supermarkets and processed foods, to appreciate the wide-ranging impact of man's learning to cultivate rather than to chase his food supply.

Permanent settlements, the forerunners of today's cities, became possible, the family system was modified, civil government developed, life became more secure, division of labor appeared, trade and commerce emerged. And population size began to increase. From 8,000 B.C. to 1650 A.D. the world's population grew from the current size of New York City, about 10 million, to that of today's India, approximately 500 million. It had taken one to two million years to achieve a human population of half a billion. If that same rate of growth had continued, the world's population would have reached 3½ billion in another seven to fourteen million years. But the rate of growth exploded in 1650, and the world's population reached 3½ billion in the late 1960s, only three hundred years later, and it is expected to add another 3½ billion in the last three decades of this century.

THE POPULATION EXPLODES

What produced this rapid growth after 1650? That's a fairly simple question to answer—the Industrial Revolution.

Whereas the Agricultural Revolution had freed man from the arbitrary whims of nature, the Industrial Revolution harnessed the forces of nature. Suddenly man no longer worked and lived in direct contact with nature. As industries grew in size and complexity, necessitating more workers in concentrated areas, so did medical and sanitary technology develop. Death rates in the industrializing nations began to drop while birth rates remained at their previously high levels. An explosion is defined by the physicist as a rapid acceleration. That is exactly the effect on population size of the Industrial Revolution. That effect, however, has not been confined to Western, industrial nations but has spread around the globe. Death rates have fallen precipitously in developing nations as swamps have been sprayed with D.D.T. and immunization has been widely adopted. The net result of it all has been to overburden the political and biological systems which had performed reasonably well at sustaining their more or less stationary populations. As the excess of births over deaths increase in the developing nations of Africa, Asia and South America, hunger, frustration and anger grow apace.

The population of Kuwait in Southwest Asia is currently growing at the unbelievable rate of 7.6 percent each year. At this rate the population will double in only nine years, subjecting this tiny nation to stresses never before experienced by any society. Neighboring Jordan is growing by 4.1 percent annually and will double in only 17 years. This phenomenal rate of growth is not unrelated to the continuing hostilities between Jews and Arabs in the Mid-East. As the Arab population grows, their need for Jewish land increases. Closer to home, Costa Rican population is expanding at a rate which would double its population every 18 years. The Philippines will double in 20 years.[3]

Americans are accustomed to thinking of these areas of the world as overpopulated, and the blame is usually laid to the high birth rate of the underdeveloped nations. The fact is that fertility rates in the poorer nations have not increased over the past several centuries, and for the past few decades some have actually shown a decline. The mushrooming population of this part of the world is a direct outgrowth of the introduction of Western medicine which drastically lowered the death rate.

America has shared its medicines with the world, thinking that by so doing it was saving millions of people from early death, and so it was. Both moral considerations and political interests seemed to profit from such an action, and it is not often that such a combination is possible. But apparently we had not done our arithmetic. For if we had, we could have seen the ruinous path on which we had embarked. American medicine, while it lowered infant mortality and lessened the ravages of plague and epidemic, unleashed the diseases of medical progress—overpopulation and its deadly accompaniments.

We were operating on a foundation of mistaken morality which made keeping people alive an end in itself. We innoculated, immunized and sprayed, and we felt good about our actions. But this self-congratulation would have been short-lived had we stuck around long enough to witness the long-term effects of our soft-hearted interference. Help and run was our philosophy, death control our objective, overpopulation the result. Motivated by a benevolent ignorance of social forces and human desires, America played unintentional havoc with the destinies of nations and peoples.

In late 1969 President Nixon congratulated the U.S. Agency for International Development (AID) for their 100 millionth smallpox vaccination in Africa. The President said, "This 100 millionth vaccination against smallpox is not only an impressive measure of technical assistance, it is 100 million opportunities to be productive citizens of Africa." [4] But opportunity is not accomplishment, and these 100 million are likely to become the lingering victims of overpopulation, inhabitants of the twilight zone between being alive and living. The African death rate is now the highest in the world, more than double that of America. As the death rate falls under the influence of Western medicine, overpopulation will severely burden Africa's attempt to join the twentieth century.

Overpopulation is a child whose teeth decay, whose bones are malformed, whose eyesight goes uncorrected and whose education is sporadic and totally inadequate for today's world. It is a body stunted by vitamin deficiency and beset by diseases unknown to the less crowded. It is a mind caged in a primitive world and dominated by the strong, where those ethics by which civilization maintains itself are irrelevant to the brutal demands of daily living.

America took two centuries to develop its medical technology. It came in small doses, with long periods of time during which the birth rate could accommodate itself to a slowly declining death rate. The life-support system of any modern society, made up of industrialization, a sophisticated food technology, specialized social relationships and a viable urbanization developed along with American medical technology. Following World War II, however, Western medicine was foisted upon peoples and nations with none of the necessary supports for a growing population. In some parts of the world death rates were cut in half in only a decade, and sometimes without the consent or knowledge of the governments affected. Thus it is both untrue and irresponsible for Americans, when discussing foreign countries, to talk about "their" population problem. It is our problem, first of all because it's a product of our science, and secondly because we have far more to lose if it is not solved. In trying for Cinderella we have created a Frankenstein.

In his book *People! Challenge to Survival*, William Vogt says:

> The resources of CARE and UNICEF are hardly likely to begin to meet the human demands of the next generation, *a generation they have helped to swell.* If hundreds of thousands, and even millions, of children starve it will be in part because of the good intentions of these organizations. They have been conspicuously unwilling to do anything about trying to reduce the birth rate.[5]

War, hunger, disease, illiteracy, political instability—all are directly related to runaway population growth. The Japanese initiated their part of World War II largely because of their rapidly growing population. Japan had 72 million people in 1940. After losing the war and some of its off-shore islands in 1945, Japan found itself with better than 90 million people in a country smaller than the state of Montana. So severe was its population problem that in 1948 Japan passed the Eugenics Protection Act which legalized and encouraged abortions. In the 10 years that followed, Japan cut its birth rate in half. Yet in 1969 Japan had 102 million people, half as many as the United States, but living on one twenty-fifth as much land. In the Western world, Japan is usually held up as the shining example of an Asian country that licked the population problem. That is absurd. Japanese farmers are among the best in the world and the land is intensively farmed. But the Japanese produce only 80 percent of their rather severe diet. Tokyo, the world's largest city with 11 million people, is also the world's most polluted city. *Newsweek* reported in 1969 that "Tokyo traffic policemen must regularly return to headquarters for oxygen inhalation." Vending machines offer the man in the street a whiff of oxygen for 25 cents, and school children wear gauze masks on smog-alert days.[6] If this is an example of success, God help the failure.

It was in large part the need for more land to provide homes and food for its people which caused Japan to invade Manchuria in 1933, thereby setting the world on a collision course with universal war. Today the spectre of 700 million Chinese, regimented and made militant by their poverty, hangs like the drawstrings of a shroud over an affluent and myopic West now flagellating itself for its former sins of omission.

World Health News reported in August 1960:

> This birthquake—this population explosion—is the greatest problem we are facing in the world today; it is greater than the ideological threats. It is largely the reason for much of the fear, the anxiety, the lack of

> physical resistance that are responsible for the deterioration in the mental health of the peoples of Asia.

The number of hungry people in the world today is greater than the total number of people alive in 1900. The continents of Africa, Asia and South America are losing the race with illiteracy, food production and political stability. The last five years have demonstrated to Americans the illusory nature of what we once called a food surplus. Experts are now predicting a worldwide food shortage by the mid 1970s and the spectre of worldwide nuclear war generated from unremitting population pressures constantly haunts us. In discussing the conclusions of a panel of eminent biologists on population growth, the *Population Bomb Newsletter* for March 1967 commented:

> All of the panelists were troubled by the fact that five nations now have the nuclear bomb. As food population pressures rise, they contended, the more will be the impulse toward war among the powers trying to control sources of supply.

The Chinese word for peace is "ho-ping" which, translated literally, means "food for all."

Ten years ago the poorest nations of the world were called "underdeveloped." Today we call them "developing" and "emerging," not because they are, but because we seem to think a progressive verb makes a progressive nation. Apparently believing that renaming a thing can automatically reduce its problem potential, we blithely label our social strychnine as essence of peppermint.

At its current growth rate of 2.5 percent India's population will pass the one billion mark in the mid-1990s. In 1969 alone it gained 13 million people, as many as all the developed countries combined. Already without homes, schooling or jobs for its urban masses, and with no possibility of improvement for the wretched poverty of its rural millions, India simply cannot survive without immediate and drastic action.

Family planning programs will not be sufficient. India has had official birth control programs since 1951, but with no success. Paul Ehrlich, Stanford University Professor of Biology, says: "At the start of the program the Indian population growth rate was around 1.3% per year, and the population was some 370 million. After 16 years of effort at family planning, the growth rate was pushing 3% per year and the population was well over 500 million." [7]

THE AMERICAN EXPERIENCE

However, I have written this book for Americans and about America. It is designed to be bought by those of you fortunate enough to have the money to spend on something less immediate than staying alive one more day and lucky enough to have attended a school which taught you to read. Unless we act soon to bring the number of Americans in line with our political and ecological ability to support human life, fewer and fewer people may find themselves able to purchase or read this or any other book. Life will have become much too frantic for such leisurely pursuits.

Even though the population problems facing the rest of the world defy adequate description, much less solution, those facing this nation are no less serious. In fact I would say that our condition is far worse, and for two reasons. The first is that we simply refuse to recognize the fact that we have a problem. The symptoms of our plight—pollution, noise, alienation, crime, loss of purpose, riots, unemployment, inadequate schools, power shortages, and so forth—though eventually fatal to any society, are more subtle and less disturbing than the wars and the starvation which now afflict the world community.

In a perceptive essay on "Urbanism As a Way of Life," Louis Wirth over 30 years ago described the psychological and sociological metamorphosis undergone by American society as it was urbanized.[8] As the nineteenth century began, slightly more than one American in twenty lived in urban areas. By

1960, the figure was seven out of ten and it continues to increase to a predicted 95 percent by the year 2000.

The American stereotype of farmers as hicks and bumpkins and city dwellers as urbane and sophisticated was certainly an exaggeration but not completely in error. The rural environment was more open and trusting. People were known by name and history. If gossip and ridicule occasionally found the wrong target, they nevertheless bound the rural community together and maintained its sense of values. The crises of life, birth, death and marriage were met and mastered by the people, with little need for "outside" help.

As Americans moved to the city in response to industrialization and their own growing numbers, most of this changed. No longer did they spend their time among those who had long known them. Trust was not so easily given or gained. Openness and sharing were casualties of the punctuality and fractionality of urban work. The control of behavior, no longer manageable by opinion and reputation, passed to police departments and professional managers. Community itself was lost as diverse racial, religious, economic, ethnic and social groups crowded in upon each other, all demanding that things be done their way. Bureaucracies operated by the book became custodians of the public welfare.

For almost a decade I have tried to teach students about the differences in rural and urban places. But not until an episode my family calls "Admire vs. St. Louis" did these differences really come through to me.

My family and I had arrived in St. Louis for the weekend, intending to see a ball game, have a picnic, visit the zoo and stay overnight in a motel. I had forgotten to bring any money with me, but I was confident I could cash a check. "I'm sorry, sir, but we accept only cash," said the ticket-seller at Busch Stadium. And even though there were thousands of empty seats in the park and I had personalized checks and all kinds of identification, I could not buy a ticket. Following this we went to a motel and tried in vain to get a room. Several service stations whose credit cards I held also refused either to cash a check or to give me money on the card. Finally at one o'clock in the morning, we found a policeman who directed us to a run-down inner-city hotel which would cash a check. But only for five dollars more than the room cost.

That five dollars was consumed for breakfast the next morning, our first meal in 18 hours. The final indignity of this unhappy trip came later that morning when I walked up to a bank teller and asked to cash a check. "Do you have an account here?" she asked. When I said, "No," her reply was, "I'm sorry, sir, we only cash checks for customers." After pleading with the bank's vice-president and offering to let him call my bank at my expense, I was finally able to cash a small check. We left St. Louis feeling like incompetent con-men.

Several years later we were driving across Kansas on the turnpike when I glanced down at the gas gauge. It was sitting on empty, and we had just passed the last gas station for 57 miles. Just then a road sign appeared announcing "Admire Exit-No Services." Hoping to find a service station somewhere, I wheeled off the toll-road and pulled to a stop at the gate. "Any chance of getting some gas around here?" I asked. " 'Bout five miles from here. Turn left at the end of this road, go three miles and turn left again. Then straight ahead a mile and a half and another left. There'll be a station on your left. But it's closed. The fella that owns it lives next door though, and he'll sell you some gas."

We found the station, but the house next door was dark and no one responded to my knock. I made my way to another house down the road. "Oh, he's gone to visit his mother," the lady explained. "You go down this road, turn right, then three blocks and turn left. There'll be a station on the right. But it's closed. I'll call Jim, though, and he'll meet you there."

We soon found the second station and the owner appeared. He unlocked the station, turned on all the lights, wiped our windshield, checked the oil, then asked, "Fill 'er up?" When I tried to pay him for his trouble, he refused, saying, "I'm here to help." We left Admire feeling like visiting dignitaries.

The founders of our country believed that the strength of

this nation rested in its rural communities and its farmers. Thomas Jefferson despised the manners and morals of the urban crowd and prayed that they would not be imported to America. The American writer, Ralph Waldo Emerson, captured this anti-urban perspective in the 1850s:

> I always seem to suffer some loss of faith on entering cities. They are great conspiracies: the parties are all maskers, who have taken mutual oaths of silence not to betray each other's secret and to keep the other's madness in countenance.

President Theodore Roosevelt appointed the Country Life Commission in 1908 for the purpose of describing the virtues of the rural life and enticing people either to stay or to return. From the activities of this Commission grew the Back-to-the-Country Movement which, until World War I, was somewhat successful. Since that time however, the pressure of numbers and the promise of a better life has swept millions from rural to urban. For the majority it has been a fool's bargain too quickly made and not easily broken. A 1970 Gallup Poll found that six out of ten adults living in urban areas would like to move from the city if they could live anywhere they wished. A similar poll taken in 1966 showed a slightly lower percentage of city dwellers who wanted to abandon it, indicating a growing disillusionment with megalopolis.[9] With the crime rate growing even faster than our population, with apathy and alienation native to our sprawling metropolises, with racial hatred diverting our ambition and corrupting our purpose, with costs and casualties mounting and no end in sight, who would rise to dispute them?

The cancer of runaway population growth has eaten away both heart and soul of the body politic. We are on the verge of anarchy with only our will to survive and our determination to act staying our fall.

If, as a nation and as individuals, we can summon the intelligence and the courage to bring population growth under control, we will find ourselves still faced with problems of race relations, crime, alienation, apathy, environmental degradation, and so forth, but with one big difference. The problems will then be capable of solution, whereas now they are not.

Population Growth and the Crime Problem Crime rates in America are skyrocketing, growing even faster than population. During the decade of the sixties, crime increased by 148 percent while population went up by 12.6 percent. During 1969 alone, crime was up 11 percent while population increased by one percent. In both cases, crime grew better than 10 times faster than population size. It is not accidental that increases in crime rates go hand in hand with population growth. Further evidence of this is the fact that crime rates are higher in urban areas than in rural areas.[10]

All creatures flourish in certain environments. Just as the crocodile is native to the swamp, and cactus grows in the desert, so the criminal finds his most hospitable surroundings in megalopolis. Here the stranger is not so noticeable nor his behavior so obvious. Potential victims are in greater abundance and hiding places more numerous. Detection, apprehension and conviction are less likely, once again due to the great number of people. While crime in the sixties increased more than 140 percent, the clearance rate for crimes declined more than 30 percent. Police clear a crime when they have identified the offender, have sufficient evidence to charge him and actually take him into custody.

The clearance rate for crimes in the United States now stands at under 25 percent. Less than one arrest is made for every four crimes committed. Of those arrested, approximately one-half are convicted by the courts, which means that seven of every eight crimes goes unpunished, and more criminals are on the street than in prison.

Can the individual policeman then, be blamed for treating everyone he arrests as if he were already guilty? Can the public be faulted for their increasingly hostile and uncooperative attitude toward the police? As an act of individual survival, the policeman must assume guilt until innocence is proven. In so doing, however, he loses the trust of the average citizen on which, in the last analysis, enforcement of the law depends.

Consider this encounter between the police and the public. In early 1970, two California state police cars pulled into a cafe parking lot to make a routine check of the cars there. With their guns holstered, two patrolmen approached an occupied car. Before they knew what was happening, they were shot dead on the spot. The other two patrolmen jumped from their car to help and were cut down by shotgun blasts. Four policemen lay dead. All across the country the next day policemen must have been more cautious, less hesitant to pull a gun. And the public response is, "Police brutality," and "The only good pig is a dead pig."

As population grows, crimes are increasingly difficult to detect and determent is impossible. As a result, harsher laws are passed and greater force is used while simultaneously public confidence declines and unrest mounts. Such are the causes of riot and revolution, anarchy and despotism.

The whole basis of classical criminology rested on the assumption that punishment of crime would be swift, certain, severe and uniform. This was always more an ideal than a reality, but today, it is an impossibility. To catch a crook in a city of half a million to 10 million is like finding the witch at a Halloween party, and even if he should be caught, the court docket is so loaded with cases that he may wait years before trial.

William Denver, Mayor of Chicago, writing in the *American Bar Association Journal* in 1926, described the beginning of what today is a crucial problem:

> . . . prompt trials are impossible with an insufficient number of criminal court judges. In Cook County . . . we have not had at any time within the last twenty years a sufficient number of criminal court judges to promptly dispose of the constantly increasing number of criminal cases.[11]

Apart from the problems of sheer numbers, a big population produces more crime for another reason. It is impossible for all those who live in a big city to understand the motivation of those who make their laws. It is also impossible for those who make the laws to give equal weight to the wishes and interests of all the people. The result is to create suspicion and resentment between citizen and lawmaker. The law is no longer seen as legitimate by the people, and the only thing that ensures their observance of it is the ability of the law enforcers to intimidate or coerce them.

The debate in Congress of programs for safe streets and crime prevention misses the mark. No amount of money or rhetoric can sufficiently restore the trust of Americans in their legal system apart from a rediscovery of the individual by the system, and this rediscovery can occur only if population growth is brought to a halt.

Dense numbers of people can transform the most common occurrence into stark tragedy and make victims of innocent passers-by. In March 1970, the nation's newspapers carried this story:

"New York—A transit policeman's attempt to give a derelict a summons for smoking in a subway yesterday touched off a shooting spree in the crowded Times Square area.

"The transit policeman and the derelict were killed, two other persons were wounded and hundreds of bystanders were forced to rush for cover. Amid the firing and the cries, crowds of shoppers and sightseers scurried for doorways and parked cars. . . ." [12]

Superfluous People Mass society lives off its productive population, those roughly between the ages of 18 and 65. The urban world has little use for the young and the old. Because they are needed later to man its industries and fight its wars, society enrolls its young in specialized institutions designed to equip them for their adult roles. Once upon a time it was thought (and occasionally practiced) that the educational experience of the young should expand their minds, develop their potential to perceive and create, teach them to entertain themselves, others and a new idea. But the big school, from pre- to graduate-, made necessary by the many people, becomes a factory turning out replacements; emphasizing uniformity rather than uniqueness, utility instead of universality. Education is made an economic decision, its soundness judged by its contribution to the gross national product.

The old are another story. Their contribution lies in the past, and they are forever, rather than temporarily useless. Because a growing population is unstable, it must make frequent changes in its ways of relating and doing. Old people are equipped by virtue both of biology and sociology for continuity rather than change. An expanding population has no place for its past; no time for the old. A fourth-grade youngster was listening to the conversation between her mother and a weekend guest they had just picked up at the airport. As they neared home, the guest pointed to the imposing old building set a hundred yards or so from the highway. "And what is that?" she asked. Before her mother could reply, the child answered, "That's where they store old people." That a small child could pass such judgment on a home for the elderly is a bitter indictment of our society. That both adults laughed at her remark reflects the lack of intelligence and compassion which characterizes our treatment of the old.

In a smaller population both the young and the old fill roles essential to the well-being of the whole. In America today, the young and the old are superfluous. But they are increasing. From 1880 to 1940, the percentage of dependent children (under 15) decreased steadily. Since 1940 the percentage has been rising and now stands at approximately 30 percent. The dependent aged (over 65) have increased steadily since 1880 and now comprise about 10 percent of the population.

Mass society has made man the "creature" obsolete by emphasizing man the "creator." Because he is not omniscient or omnipotent, man as creator has a much shorter life expectancy than man the creature. The relentless increase in knowledge dooms the creator to a very short existence. Both before he acquires the ability to create and after he loses it (by doing it as he was taught rather than as the young are doing it) man is without purpose—superfluous.

We wax sentimental about babies and grandparents, teenagers and golden-agers, but sentiment is not respect nor is nostalgia negotiable. Because human value in mass society is utilitarian rather than inherent, it generates an endless and increasing supply of useless people.

It is in large part the future which the young protest as well as the present. The security of longer life expectancy has been offset by the fear of disabling illness, inadequate income and a parasitic existence. The old are unwanted and unhappy. If the old had the energy and had not been sold a bill of goods over their lifetime about the joys of retirement, they too might be violent. In addition to campus disorders, we could have retirement revolts. To the Students for a Democratic Society could be added the G.S.D.—the Geriatrics for Self-Determination.

Mass society not only makes superfluous people of its young and old but a sizable portion of its "productive" population as well. The American economic system operates on the premise that full employment would be ruinous. The reasoning goes something like this: If everyone in the work force had a job, labor could demand and get whatever it wanted. Since there would be no surplus workers from which management could draw replacements, there would be nothing to hold labor's demands for higher wages in check. Runaway inflation would be the result. Thus the unemployed segment of the labor force keeps the economy going and maintains the balance between labor and management.

Economists tell us that approximately four percent of the labor force must be deprived of work for this reason. The larger the labor force, the greater the number of the unemployed. There were approximately four and a half million Americans unemployed in mid-1970, and the number is rising. Rather than gratitude for their public service, the unemployed are made to feel guilty because they do not work. They are told they are useless, and that is how they feel and act.

But even those who work today are largely superfluous. The American factory and industrial worker exercises almost no initiative in his work. All of his working life is played out in a coercive environment in which he is told what to do and when and how to do it, either by big business or by big unions. The worker is socialized to respond, with little or no reflection on his part, to commands and cues from those who control his livelihood and thereby his life. We cannot reasonably expect man reduced to manikin proportions as a latent function of his employment to assume an interest, much less a position of leadership, in community affairs. Political and social passivity may thus be seen as causally related to the bureaucratic rationality which American industry applies.

Henry Anderson is 33 years old, married and the father of three children. He grew up in rural Missouri, and although he finished high school, his education is inferior when measured against today's job market. He lives in a suburb of Kansas City where he has worked for the past six years in an automobile assembly plant. Henry normally works 10 hours a day, six days a week. But his foreman can demand, with no advance notice, that he work 12 hours a day, seven days a week, in order to meet increased production schedules. At least once a year Henry is put out of work altogether by change-over from one model to another.

Henry takes no part in community affairs. Though his brother in California is a minister and another relative is a teacher, Henry expresses no interest in anything. He rarely sees his neighbors and only infrequently takes his wife out. He is a stranger to his children, a visitor in his own home. Henry works to live and lives to work, but he finds little purpose and no pleasure in any of it. Increasingly he sees his family and his employer as leeches, draining his life for their own benefit. His community is an alien and hostile world, frustrating his ambitions and dwarfing his interests. Henry is a victim of industrial rationality.

Industry, however, has not applied such rationality by choice but by necessity. Efficiency charts, time clocks, assembly lines and many of the other trappings of our industrial process were imposed upon workers in an effort to supply the necessities and satisfy the desires of a growing population. The growing population in turn forced the worker to greater specialization and division of labor. Whereas the worker once had been a craftsman, putting hand and heart into a unique product, he became a station on a conveyor belt, performing a monotonous chore on a monotonous product. As his work lost meaning, his life lost purpose; the worker withdrew from community affairs and abandoned his convictions. He became an anonymous member of the Silent Majority, used on occasion by politicians, tested now and then by pollsters, but in general, superfluous. It used to be that more people were necessary to fill a constantly expanding job market—jobs which were essential to community and national welfare. Now more jobs are necessary to keep up with a constantly growing population. And these jobs are often deadend, make-work jobs, the sole purpose of which is to keep the worker busy.

Apathy and Alienation A fascinating book appeared in 1950. Called *The Lonely Crowd* and subtitled, *A Study of the Changing American Character*, this book relates size and rate of growth of the United States population to the changing personality of its people. The authors maintain that members of a society are directed [controlled] in one of three ways: (1) by tradition, (2) by an inner sense of right and wrong, or (3) by others. Where the direction comes from depends upon the size and rate of growth of the population.[13]

In early societies with their high birth and death rates and resulting slow rate of growth the people were directed in their daily activities by tradition. The past became present to shape the future. So long as population growth was at a snail's pace, the customary institutions and patterns of behavior were sufficient to handle whatever problems arose. After all, the problems were the same as those faced by the previous generation, and the one before it, as far back as anyone could remember.

Life for early societies was not always pleasant or easy, but it was highly predictable. People knew what to expect, though they might have wished differently had they ever known things to be different.

But then death rates began to drop while birth rates remained at their previously high levels. The resulting population increase upset the balance long governed by custom and tradition. Change in size produced change in attitude. Accepted ways of relating to other people and to the environment no longer were sufficient. Longevity ceased to be the criterion for legitimacy. The dead hand of the past became the open mind of the present. The motivation for individual lives was now conviction rather than tradition. Each person decided for himself what music he was to heed and what, if any, cause he was to take up.

As population size increased from a very small base and at a somewhat manageable rate, it was possible to maintain this inner-directed man who knew who he was and what he was about. Over the last half century, however, population growth has been so rapid and the size so great that the inner-directed man, like the earlier tradition-directed, has become a rare, if not extinct, variety of *homo sapiens*.

His place has been assumed by the other directed individual, the organization man, the social chameleon who takes on the protective opinions and habits of his associates. As our numbers and our things become bigger, the individual becomes smaller. From being an individual in a community, he becomes an infinitesimal bit of living matter in the vastness of the city, the government, the organization. He becomes a string of numbers, a series of roles. He is reduced from flesh and blood to computer tape, from hopes and fears to a case study, from uniqueness to uniformity. As a group of people becomes larger in size, the number of possible relationships in which they might participate expands even faster. James Bossard developed a formula for predicting the number of potential relationships in various size groups.[14] Using his formula, $\frac{N^2 - N}{2}$, where "N" equals the number of people, we arrive at the following:

NUMBER OF PEOPLE	NUMBER OF POSSIBLE RELATIONSHIPS
2	1
3	3
4	6
5	10
6	15
7	21
8	28
9	36
10	45
25	300
100	4,950
1,000,000	499,999,500,000

As the number of possible relationships between people increases, so does personal insecurity growing from unknown persons and situations. Just the effort required to initiate and sustain the necessary interpersonal relationships is enough to frighten many people. Modern Americans live with millions of others, yet know only a handful. Suspicion and anonymity are essential for social survival but deadly for the spirit and the psyche.

It is inevitable that population increases make it ever more difficult to know the individual. And when the individual is unknown, the society is suspected. As the difficulty of knowing the person increases, the sophistication of snooping, and the use of it, necessarily grows. Politically and psychologically the individual suffers in mass society. Those who oppose in the name of freedom, measures designed to control population size thereby insure the loss of that freedom.

The result of this depersonalization of the individual has been either withdrawal or protest. For millions of people surrender has been their only escape. They do not vote, for what does one man's opinion matter in an electorate of thousands or millions? They do not participate in community affairs, first because they believe the system to be rigged in favor of the monied and the powerful; secondly, because they have no feeling for the place in which they find themselves. They are only migrants, moved about by giant corporations and warring nations like pawns on a chessboard. They dare not put down roots lest the pain of forced withdrawal do them in. They substitute contrived conviviality, the artificially created camaraderie of strangers, for friendship. They pay for their two cars and three bedrooms with induced unfeeling. They are emotional delinquents rewarded by the system for their uncaring pliability.

While flying from Dallas to Fargo several years ago, I found myself engrossed in conversation with a bright young man whose name, Dick Slade, would have done justice to a dimestore novel and whose philosophy of work was a succinct commentary on the ethics of a business society.

After telling me how he hated big business and big cities—particularly Chicago—he followed up by announcing that he had just gone to work for a national computer company in Chicago. When I suggested some slight inconsistency in his statements, he replied, "But that's where the security is—the big company. You can get ahead with them, but you have to go where they say. Of course my wife doesn't want to leave North Dakota, but she has no choice. I could have stayed with my home-town job, but there're a small company and you can't count on them. Anyway they don't reward talent. I was the best salesman they had. All the promotions went to the so-and-so's who kissed the boss's rear end.

"Anyway, I don't plan to live in Chicago. I can't—already I've developed an allergy. Only been there a week but that air is filthy. Not fit to breathe. I'll live 40 or 50 miles out and take the train in. I don't know how I'll afford a house though. Looked at several modest homes. In North Dakota they'd cost 9 to 14 thousand, in Chicago they're 20 thousand and up.

"One of these days, though, in a year or two, I can bid out

and make it back to Minneapolis. Till then we'll just have to roll with the punches."

I parted from Mr. Dick Slade thinking that I had just spent an hour with the All-American Man.

But there is another group! These refuse to conform or to withdraw. They are not apathetic but alienated. They seek not to escape but to engage, not to conform but to confront.

Protest has assumed epidemic proportions. Violence and vileness characterize all our relationships, from the P.T.A. to the S.D.S., from Chicago to Berkeley, from insult to insurrection, from hope to despair.

The issues which motivate and the tactics which direct the ever growing number of protest organizations are beyond counting. The poor and the black young feel cheated because they have never had a piece of the action. They want in. Affluent white youth are turned off by the organization man and the status seekers. They want out. As different as both groups are in their perspective on what they disdainfully call "the establishment," they share a common desire to change it.

Welfare Rights, Black Power, Chicano, Equality of the Sexes, relevant education, war and peace, capitalism, burgeoning bureaucracy, abortion, religion, sex education, racism, environmental degradation, the population explosion, crime—these are only a partial listing from the catalogue of alienation. And the number increases as human numbers expand.

Both apathy and alienation are eventually fatal for any society. If we are to resurrect community from chaos, strength from weakness, unity from division, we must face the fact that our bigness has surpassed our ability to accommodate it. Overpopulation saps the strength of a society as overweight does for the individual.

As human beings crowd in upon each other, privacy becomes a luxury which only the rich can approximate, but even they cannot attain. The housing complex rising hundreds of feet into the air provides sleeping and eating space for urban man. Separated from others above, below and on all sides by a poorly insulated wall, urban man performs his most private acts. From his compartment, he scurries each morning to an even bigger and more complex edifice, frequently employing more people than lived in the community from which he came. For eight long hours he labors among those he never knew and is afraid to meet. He works to afford his apartment in which he lives to be near his work. At night he retreats to his living space seeking an elusive solitude which, if he is of rural origin, he remembers from his childhood, and, if of urban upbringing, because man can remain human only if he occasionally can be alone with himself.

In such surroundings man becomes less than human. The city creates its own deviates. A recent book by Desmond Morris described the city as *The Human Zoo*. In the wild, animals do not kill for pleasure, are not homosexual, do not confuse their sexual identities, and they understand how they are to relate to their own kind. In captivity, however, these same animals kill without need, become sexual perverts, and no longer understand how they should relate to those about them. So the city affects man.[15]

In his studies of experimental animals, John Calhoun documented the "behavioral sink" which operates as population density increases. Calhoun defines the behavioral sink as "the outcome of any behavioral process that collects animals together in unusually great numbers. The unhealthy connotations of the term are not accidental: behavioral sink does act to aggravate all forms of pathology that can be found within a group."[16]

The pathology associated with density was most pronounced in the female. She often would not carry pregnancy to full term, and if she did, was likely to die herself. The mothers who survived were usually unable to nurse their young, and infant mortality reached 80 percent. Females also lost their biologically necessary ability to build nests. Density would have wiped out the entire population if the experiments had continued long enough, by causing the reproductive function to fail.

The male also experienced behavioral disturbances: sexual deviation, cannibalism, overactivity, withdrawal from community life and disruption of the social organization. Sexual combinations took on unusual forms. Calhoun commented: "One group might consist of six or seven females and one male, whereas another would have 20 males and only 10 females." [17]

If human numbers continue to mount, trampling privacy and personality in their scramble for survival, man himself will be reduced to an experimental animal on whom a similar verdict may one day be rendered.

Birth and Taxes The saying goes that nothing is inevitable in life except death and taxes. That statement should be amended, because it is also inevitable that births drive taxes higher. Population growth is the greatest generator of the increased cost of government, a cost paid by all of us in the form of taxation. Taxes may be defined as the decision to spend money publicly rather than privately. Such public spending must be constantly increased to build schools, roads, sewers, water lines, recreational facilities, prisons, housing projects, and other necessities and amenities for a growing population.

Every citizen in a community, whether he has children or not, is forced to assume the burden for those who do. For the cost of child-rearing is borne in large measure by the community, not the parents. Average middle income parents pay from $15,000 to $25,000 in out-of-pocket expenses to rear a child from birth to 18 years of age. This is a sizable sum, but it's only a fraction of the total cost; the remainder is apportioned among the citizens of the community in the form of taxes.

The typical suburban parents of three children spend from one to four thousand dollars a year (depending mostly upon the age of the children) in direct costs—food, clothing, health care, travel, and so forth. They spend another one to two thousand dollars in taxes to care for the children of the community. The indirect costs of parenthood are in addition to this. Bigger houses and cars, higher utility bills, more frequent repairs and replacement of appliances and tools, and perhaps the biggest indirect cost of all—the father's commuting to work. Middle-income families have been moving to the suburbs in increasing numbers ever since World War II. As the city became increasingly less attractive, those who were able, by virtue of income and color, sought sanctuary in the suburbs. In an effort to escape rising taxes and declining services, and to recapture some of the simplicity of the rural environment, young parents took their children to the trees and fresh air of the suburbs. Father paid for the family's hideaway in tiring hours of travel to work and hundreds of dollars per year in transportation charges.

The irony is that the conditions which middle-income Americans sought to escape by moving from the city are now invading the suburbs. The trees are bulldozed to make room for monotonous, mass-produced houses and an increasing number of high-rise apartment buildings. The fresh air is clouded by the factories which also are fleeing the rising taxes, poor transportation and inadequate city services. The interstate highway development of circumvential and radial routes has displaced the inner city as a business and industrial center. The economic and human viability of all big American cities is declining and will continue to do so. The only thing leaving the ghetto and the slum bound for the suburbs are the jobs once available to those who lived in the inner city.

Suburbanites are finding it increasingly difficult to finance the rapid growth of their communities. The tax bill keeps climbing, but not so fast as the need for expanded medical facilities, public schools, streets, police and fire protection. The only way the suburbs can come close to public financial solvency is to expand their tax base, increase their tax rate, or both. But family dwellings and members are not a sufficient source of public funds; only industry pays more in taxes than it consumes. So suburban Chambers of Commerce vie with one another for industries.

Thus middle-class Americans and their jobs have abandoned the city for the suburbs only to restart the cycle of events which prompted their pilgrimage. Who is to say that birth and taxes are not inevitable?

The Ugliness of Utility Urban renewal, interstate highways, slum clearance, model cities, housing developments, subdivisions, all are break-neck attempts to keep up with the population avalanche. Under the sheer weight of numbers, the face of our nation has lost its cherubic glow and its inviting manner. Like the head of Medusa, the physical appearance of Modern America turns the heart to stone. Commercial ugliness assaults natural beauty on every hand. Legislatures, courts, administrative bodies and big business—all conspire, either from ignorance or from vested interest, to modify and mutilate the only land we'll ever have.

Old buildings are torn down to make way for new ones. Just as the megalopolis has no place for old people, it has no use for old buildings. "Everything's up-to-date in Kansas City" brags the Chamber of Commerce, and to make it so we tear down our past. Gone are the old hotels where presidents and kings once stayed; in their place, a parking lot and a hamburger joint. Landmarks give way to neon signs. Scenic drives become super-highways. The inner city is cut to pieces by a staggering assortment of cloverleafs, overpasses, tunnels, high-speed interchanges, over-large bridges, cross-walks and access roads, all giving the appearance of a spaghetti bowl flung from a giant hand. The American dilemma of the 1970s is how to get somewhere, yet have something to see when we arrive. In our efforts to get there faster and in greater numbers, we often destroy the reason for going.

Our cities raze their cultural and historical attractions to erect giant hotels and sprawling motor-inns in order to accommodate the thousands of tourists who come to see the cultural and historical attractions. If this makes no sense to you, then you aren't thinking big. And God knows, Americans think big. Our national parks have become so accessible and so utilized that they differ little from luxury motels. In a three-week trip through the Southeast several years ago, I found my family had to have reservations for a place to pitch a tent. The portable television sets drowned out the murmur of the brook and the chirp of the crickets. The expensive campers sitting smartly in their allotted space, conveniently connected to electricity and sewage, effectively camouflaged whatever remnants of nature remained. Some of our National parks are now so crowded that visitors are admitted by number, much like in a giant department store. Millions of Americans belong to camping, hiking and nature clubs. It's as if we had suddenly realized the imminent demise of nature and wanted to have one last fling. The old-timer of the future may well be the one who can describe to his grandchildren the bear he once saw in the Smokies or the trees in Northern California.

America is fast becoming all present, no past, and little future. If we aren't wise beyond what we have shown to date, there will soon be no life forms—animal, mineral or vegetable—to link us with our ancestors. We will be a people without a past, contemplating an uncertain and unlovely future.

A national television show not long ago milked a cow in front of millions of viewers, explaining that many in the audience had never seen it done. Middle-class Americans are hothouse creatures sustained by hybrid grains, artificial sweeteners, fluoridated water and food substitutes, cooled and warmed by mechanically treated air, commanding machines to do our work, exercising our jaw bones and writing hands. We have much, know much and do much. We make the decisions and conduct the actions which ruin our land. We direct our institutions toward maintenance of our artificially high standard of living.

Even the Church serves our purposes. It emphasizes the responsible use of personal finances and individual talents, but it completely neglects the stewardship of our earth. The Church says nothing about our wasteful economy with its planned obsolescence and profligate use of resources. It does not challenge the shortsighted "dam building syndrome" of the U.S. Corps of Engineers which destroys the natural beauty of our countryside and alters the ecological balance of nature. Litter and polution corrupt our environment, costing us billions of dollars, inflicting an incalculable loss to our aesthetic and spiritual needs, yet there is no prophet crying in this man-made desert to call us back to reason and to responsibility.

Paradise is rapidly being lost, never to be regained, yet the Church makes no protest. It is as if the Church had lost its vision of the kingdom coming on earth as it is in Heaven.

The President's Council on Recreation and Natural Beauty was right when it commented:

> No major urban center in the world has yet demonstrated satisfactory ways to accommodate growth. In many areas, expanding population is out-running the readily available supply of food, water, and other basic resources and threatens to aggravate beyond solution the staggering problems of the new urban society.[18]

4 Perspectives on Population Growth

We must now—immediately cease looking at burgeoning populations with the eyes of generations long dead.

—Margaret Mead [1]

I and several other graduate students were gathered in Professor Pihlblad's office. He was an elderly and distinguished gentleman and had just completed a very scholarly lecture on the methods of computing a life-table. As was true all semester, his classroom presentation was thorough, sophisticated and very theoretical. Never did he allow himself to become emotional about the subject of population. He was teaching us to be professional demographers. But in the privacy of his office, his formality soon evaporated, and he became a warm human being vitally concerned about the individual and social problems related to population growth.

"You know," he said, "I've been teaching this course since I was a young man, and in that time, the population of the world has doubled. If you students and your sons teach, it will have doubled twice more." Then came the question I've never been able to escape, "What will have happened to our world?"

From that moment I was determined to be more than a technically competent population analyst. For that alone would not answer his question. It is up to all of us to determine what will have happened to this world by the time our grandchildren inherit it. I am terrified at the prospect of the 14 billion people who will share this tiny globe with our children's children unless we quickly change our attitudes and actions toward population growth.

In June, 1970 the First National Congress on Optimum Population and Environment was held in Chicago. Attending the Congress were 1200 delegates from all across the United States and a number of foreign countries. The delegates represented a variety of organizations and interests touching on questions of population and environment—League of Women Voters, Metropolitan Committee on Black Survival, Young Americans for Freedom, American Cemetery Association, *Playboy* magazine, American Institute of Architects, Zero Population Growth, Dry Cleaning and Dye House Worker's Union, Salvation Army, American Jewish Committee, the Y.M.C.A., Atomic Energy Commission, New Party of Florida, Sears Roebuck and Co., American Society of Christian Ethics, Defenders of the Fox River, Chemical Process Industry and scores of others.

The Congress was a gamble that such diverse interests could be focused on a common problem, resulting in collective action. To a degree, the gamble paid off. But to an even greater extent, the Congress laid bare the diversity of opinion and the lack of consensus on appropriate action.

The position statement presented to the Congress by the Black Caucus was symptomatic of the diverse perspectives on population growth in America. With respect to the current emphasis on population problems, the Black Caucus held that, "The appeal of a new cause can not be allowed to distract us from the unpleasant realities of today."

But population pressure is not a new cause and it cannot be divorced from problems of race, war, poverty and other social cancers. If it weren't for overpopulation, all of these would be less serious issues, because there would be enough room and resources for everyone, thus eliminating scarcity and competition which fuel these problems. If you say "scarcity" slowly and distinctly, you have "scare city," a revealing insight into the fears and frustrations of megalopolis.

Perhaps it would help if we reviewed what has been said about population size and growth in the past.

EARLY DEMOGRAPHIC THOUGHT

From antiquity it has been recognized that the size of population and level of living are reciprocals, mutual cause and effect. Confucius and other ancient Chinese philosophers stated a concept of optimum agrarian population and provided for governmental policies designed to plan the growth and distribution of population. They were also concerned with checks to population growth, such as increasing mortality, war and reduced marriage rate.[2]

Plato and Aristotle also touched upon questions of a demographic nature in their penetrating analyses of society. Like the earlier Chinese, they were interested in the optimum population, but their emphasis was not so much the limiting influence of agricultural productivity as the ideal size of population making for the "good life." Plato specified 5,040 as the number of citizens "most likely to be useful to all cities," because it has "fifty-nine divisors" and "will furnish numbers for war and peace and for all contracts and dealings, including taxes and divisions of the land." Aristotle was less specific as to the optimum size of population but argued that poverty would result if numbers and growth were not limited.[3]

Both writers gave considerable attention to methods of controlling population size. Plato proposed to restrict births by permitting only the most fit to reproduce. Public opinion and rewards would be used to encourage births; stigmas and rebuke of the young men by their elders would restrict births when necessary. If population became too large, colonization could be used to drain off the surplus, whereas immigration would replenish a population decimated by war or epidemic. Aristotle advocated putting deformed children out to die and abortion, with some discussion of eugenics, as methods of controlling population growth. He also mentioned such things as homosexuality as population checks.[4]

The Romans, in keeping with their emphasis upon the practical rather than the theoretical, devoted little attention to the consequences of population size, other than the assumed military advantage, and contented themselves with implementing policies designed to increase their progeny and thereby, their strength.[5] In this respect they resemble modern Marxist societies. The Romans viewed population in terms of empire, as the Chinese had done, rather than in relation to small city states, as the Greeks had done, and did not comprehend at all that the distribution of population was almost as important as the absolute size.

During the one thousand years separating the fall of Rome and the coming of the Renaissance, in that period labeled by various historians as the Medieval period, the Dark Ages and/or the Feudal period, most social thought of note was fashioned by the moral and ethical teachings of the Christian church as interpreted by such luminaries as St. Augustine and St. Thomas Aquinas. Population questions were viewed in the light of their religious implications. Since this life was simply preparation for the next, little attention was given to questions of material import. The latent function of the Church's teachings during this period, however, was to encourage population growth. Its condemnation of abortion, infanticide, and divorce on religious grounds resulted indirectly in population growth. But because the social doctrines of this period sprang from a concern with the theological or supernatural, we find other doctrines which served to reduce fertility. For example, the Church forbade polygamy, glorified virginity and continence, considered celibacy superior to marriage for certain persons and disapproved of second marriages.[6]

Early Medieval writers did not argue for population increase for the purpose of strengthening the state, but with the revival of Aristotle's influence in the latter part of this period, such an argument was advanced.

The United Nations' Population Division summed up the thinking of this period as follows:

> Arguments in favor of population increase predominated in the writings of European authors on population during the early modern, as well as the medieval period. The discovery of the New World, the increase of commerce between Europe and Asia, the rise of national states, and the Protestant Reformation brought some revision of the terms of discussion of population questions, but until the latter part of the eighteenth century there was no widespread change of attitude with regard to the desirability of a large and increasing population.[7]

Ibn Khaldun, an Arabian social philosopher of the fourteenth century, expounded a theory of cyclical variations of population and their relationship to economic, political and social-psychological conditions. He reasoned that densely settled population was more favorable for high per capita income than sparse population, and he thought that fertility was affected by what man believed the future held in store.[8] Khaldun's writings, although chronologically 600 years old, are modern indeed in point of view. But his works had very little influence on the East and were not widely known in the West until the twentieth century.

Botero, a sixteenth-century Italian, anticipated Malthus in several respects. He held that man's reproductive performance operated with undiminished vigor regardless of his numbers, whereas man's capacity to produce subsistence was subject to limits. Botero listed war, strife, disease and various secondary checks as products of the struggle for subsistence which operated to limit population growth.[9]

MERCANTILIST POPULATION THEORY AND POLICY

Mercantilism, the prevailing economic doctrine of Western Europe during the seventeenth and eighteenth centuries emphasized the economic and political advantages of a large and growing population.[10] It was thought that a nation's strength depended upon its having a large population to work its land, settle its colonies, fight its wars and feed the labor force consumed by its fledgling industries. This was the period of the great immigration of peoples from Europe to her far-flung colonies and also the beginning of the Industrial Revolution. Governments adopted pro-natalist policies to insure a sufficient supply of people for these purposes: the unmarried were penalized financially and socially, marriage and large families were encouraged through the offer of monetary rewards, illegitimacy was condoned.

Mercantilist writers were concerned exclusively with the welfare of the states. They were most decidedly not interested in the hardships suffered by any given family as the result of having too many children. What was good for the country and the national economy was good for the individual. It was the duty of the laboring classes, reasoned the mercantilists, to reproduce so as to maintain the supply of labor at a higher level than the demand. For unless this occurred, labor would receive too great a share of the rewards of its work, and the state would be impoverished by just that amount. As it was the individual's duty to be prolific, so it was the state's duty to see to it that the worker realized from his work only enough to enable him to work and reproduce at maximum efficiency. The "horse feed theory" argued that it was reasonable to feed a man as one would feed a horse—enough to keep him in harness but not enough to enable him to kick up his heels.

The entire political and economic structure of this period was predicated on the assumption that a perfect inverse relationship existed between the wealth of the individual and that of the nation—the poorer the individual, the richer the nation. However, mercantilism did recognize one factor which necessitated certain population limits. A central doctrine of mercantilism was the necessity for a favorable balance of trade. Any condition which endangered this balance was dangerous;

therefore, population had to maintain a level at which little or no importation of foodstuffs was necessary.

For the most part, mercantilism was not concerned with general or systematic explanation of population change, but some writers were concerned with these larger questions. Even they, however, favored population growth.

MALTHUSIAN POPULATION THEORY

Thomas Robert Malthus revolted against the Utopian schemes and the belief in the perfectibility of man's characteristic of the Western Europe of his day: Condorcet's conjectures regarding the perfectibility of man, Godwin's system of equality and his allegation that the vices of mankind originated in human institutions, Wallace's contention that overpopulation would develop only in the distant future. Malthus inveighed against them with all the clerical fervor he could muster and, with his hastily penned polemic, changed completely the character of all future concern with the population question.

Malthus' main ideas were very simply stated, but the implications were frightening as, indeed, they were meant to be. His three principal assumptions were: (1) Food is necessary to the existence of man; (2) The passion (sexual drive) between the sexes is necessary, and will not change over time; (3) The rate of population increase is indefinitely greater than the power in the earth to produce subsistence (food supply) for man.[11] Population, when unchecked, increases in a geometrical ratio, 2, 4, 8, 16, 32, 64, 128, while subsistence increases in an arithmetic ratio, 1, 2, 3, 4, 5, 6, 7.

Malthus' formulations were to form the basis, as Darwin's did a half century later, for attacks on poor laws, charity and humane treatment of the poor, as upsetting the natural order of things and leading to dangerous population increases. Malthus foresaw only famine, war, disease and other undesirable social conditions as capable of preventing a rapid increase in numbers. He recognized the existence of preventive measures such as abstention from marriage, but did not believe fertility would be greatly affected. He condemned contraception as leading to vice and argued that it would not significantly reduce fertility anyway. A good case could be made for considering Malthus' first *Essay on the Principles of Population,* written in 1798, as one of the half dozen or so most important books ever written. It was tremendously important in its impact on economic and political questions. It was only after reading it that Darwin was able to arrive at his statement of the *Origin of Species,* and it was only after exposure to Darwin's work that Marx stated his dialectic interpretation of history. We can only wonder how different the world would be today had T. R. Malthus been an illiterate Ubangi shaman rather than an erudite Anglican minister.

How accurately the views expressed in his first *Essay* reflect his own position rather than his desire to discredit his opponents, is difficult to say. In his later writings, Malthus modified his theory somewhat to admit that factors other than means of subsistence affected man's numbers, but he maintained the essential accuracy of his original statements.

The pervasive influence of Malthus may be seen by the fact that population theory is often divided into pre- and post-Malthusian and the fact that most modern demographers and population analysts identify themselves as Malthusians (rare), Anti-Malthusians (plentiful) or Neo-Malthusians (in moderate numbers but increasing).

Malthus made two serious mistakes. First he failed to foresee the widespread use of contraceptives in the Western world which was just beginning to develop in his day. He was quite right in saying that man's sexual drive would continue in the future as in the past, but he misjudged the consequences of that drive. Malthus did not make sufficient distinction between fecundity and fertility, assuming as he did that most women would actually bear as many children as biologically possible, limited only by certain cultural restrictions having to do with marriage and the family. But it has not turned out to be that simple.

Fecundity refers to the biological capacity of the female to reproduce. The human female is capable of giving birth for approximately 30 years, from about age 15 to 45. The period from conception to parturition is nine months. Allowing another nine months for recovery before another pregnancy begins, it would take a year and a half of the woman's 30-year fertility for each birth, or a total of 20 births. Most cultures do not allow marriage until some years after the development of the biological ability to reproduce. This, plus the fact that advancing age somewhat reduces fecundity, means that the maximum number of births possible to a typical human female ranges somewhere between 10 and 18. Some women, however, due to almost continuous pregnancy and multiple births, have become mothers of 30, 40 and even more children. The record is held by a European woman of last century who gave birth to 69 children: four sets of quads, seven sets of triplets and sixteen pairs of twins.

Malthus also failed to see the greatly increasing productivity of the land. The development of chemical fertilizers, pesticides, herbicides, disease-resistant crops and highly efficient farm machinery, multiplied beyond his wildest expectation the ability of the land to support human life. In his day, an American farmer did well to feed himself and his family. Today that same farmer feeds 25 to 50 people, and they are more adequately fed.

Because of these two oversights in his observations, some modern demographers dismiss Malthus completely. But they shouldn't, for though they can show that he was wrong in these particulars, they have not demonstrated his error in principle. Population in the 1970s is still outrunning food supply as it was in the 1790s. Human fertility still outstrips the fertility of the earth. Malthus may yet be right in his dire predictions of famine and war.

Herbert Spencer, writing in 1880, argued that the preservation of the species is the general biological law governing the growth of all populations.[12] Spencer posited antagonistic processes, "individuation" and "genesis," to account for the change in population size. Individuation has to do with the "power of a species to maintain and conserve the life of its individual members," [13] while genesis refers to the capacity of the species to reproduce its kind. These are antagonistic processes because they vary inversely. If they varied directly, or positively, the result would be unity or a stationary population. But neither is the relationship between them perfectly negative. For if it were, the result would be either high fertility and low mortality or high mortality and low fertility, both of which would eventually prove fatal. Spencer recognized that the relationship needed to be qualified because the power of "genesis decreases not quite so fast as individuation increases" [14] so that the result is an increase in population, the size of the increase depending upon the differential between them.

Spencer argued, contrary to Malthus, that population growth was the grand cause of human progress:

> It produced the original diffusion of the race. It compelled man to abandon predatory habits and take to agriculture. It led to the clearing of the Earth's surface. It forced men into the social state; made social organization inevitable; and has developed the social sentiments . . . And after having caused, as it ultimately must, the due peopling of the globe, and the rising of all its habitable parts into the highest state of culture—after having, at the same time, developed the intellect into complete competency for its work, and the feelings into complete fitness for social life—after having done all this, the pressure of population, as it gradually finishes its work, must gradually bring itself to an end.[15]

Spencer displayed a confidence in the operation of "natural" law which issued more from faith and hope than from reason or logic. As much as one might want to believe that the population problem will resolve itself through the working of his antagonistic processes, it must be admitted that it is impossible to find empirical evidence to support the position. His formulation assumes an ordered and conservative natural universe, the existence of which science itself is now inclined to doubt.

POPULATION DOCTRINES OF CLASSICAL ECONOMICS

The development of population theory from around 1800 to approximately 1870 was dominated primarily by two distinct and rather divergent schools of thought, the classical economists and the socialists.[16]

Classical Economic theory was concerned with the causes and consequences of population changes through its efforts to discover the "laws" governing the levels and trends of production, wages, interest, rents and profits. From their theories flowed arguments, far more sophisticated than Malthus' ratios, to support the thesis that population growth tended to depress wages and create poverty.

Laws of diminishing and increasing returns were stated; for example, John Stuart Mill's assertion that agricultural returns fall as population increases. A concept known as "stationary state," concerned with the process by which an equilibrium is established between capital formation and size of population, was much discussed. It was thought that the size of a country's population varied inversely with the per capita consumption, which in turn varies directly with the degree of inequality of incomes. Say's "law of markets" was developed as a refutation of the theory of Ortes, de Tracy, and others, which held that the demand for labor was never sufficient to afford employment to more than one-half the population. Say's thesis was that an increment in supply tended to generate its own demand.

SOCIALIST POPULATION THEORY

All socialist writers in the first two-thirds of the nineteenth century shared certain points of view toward the population problem. They all insisted that population size and rate of growth were problems only because economic and social development had not been sufficiently perfected. Once socialism were to replace capitalism, all population pressures would be relieved. But the various socialist factions did disagree on selected aspects of the population question.

The English Ricardian Socialists rejected Malthus, believing that population growth could be controlled in a cooperative society. They thought that production could keep pace with population for centuries. In fact, population growth was seen as desirable to the extent that it generated a division of labor and stimulated invention.

French Socialists rejected Malthus because of the severe implications which seemed to flow from his analysis: a denial of the bounty of nature, opposition to social reform and reorganization and a lack of happiness for the worker. Fourier believed that the establishment of the "societary state," with its physiological, dietary and other changes, would effectively control population growth. Blanc and Proudhon argued that a reorganization of society would eliminate any population problems. Loria and Nitti reasoned that population pressures were characteristic only of certain stages of economic development.[17]

Marxists also rejected Malthus. Marx did not think there was any universal law of population or that overpopulation was a function of man's biological proclivities. Overpopulation was simply the result of the capitalistic mode of production. And the population problem would disappear when Socialism replaced Capitalism, a transition which the operation of the Marxian dialectic insured. Marxism did not provide for family limitation because in a perfectly organized society, with its unlimited expansion of capital, all members are provided for.[18]

Since about 1879, the writings of non-socialists have departed more from the Malthusian viewpoint with the result that the distinction between socialist and non-socialist doctrine on the subject is no longer so distinct. *The Determinants and*

Consequences of Population Trends, published by the United Nations in 1953, lists four reasons for this convergence: (1) statistical information and methods of analysis relative to demographic phenomena have greatly improved; (2) from about 1870, fertility and mortality rates declined in certain of the economically most advanced countries, for example, the United States, England and parts of Western Europe; (3) living conditions in these countries were raised as improvements were made in manufacturing and mining industries; (4) sociology and the study of social evolution have devoted increasing attention to population study while new emphases have developed in economics.[19]

DEVELOPMENT OF MULTIPLE FACTOR THEORIES OF POPULATION GROWTH

For the most part, writers of the eighteenth and early nineteenth centuries assumed that the food supply was the sole regulator of population size. More recently, however, other factors have been recognized as playing a part in population change:

> More and more the growth of population has been treated as a function of increasing income; thus the pertinence of Malthusian theory regarding the increase of "subsistence" and its relation to population growth has diminished.[20]

Population analysts of the last 50 to 75 years have been concerned with the reasons for declining fertility rates in some European countries. R. Berini, in his 1901 *Principi di demograpia,* believed that when the earth had become sufficiently peopled, a balance of fertility and mortality would be established through the development of new marriage customs and other modifications of the social structure. John Bates Clark argued in *Essentials of Economic Theory* (1907), that the rising standard of living of developing countries was self-perpetuating, in the absence of such conditions as monopoly, war, bad government and class struggle. Pigou reasoned in his 1932 *The Economics of Welfare,* that population in modern societies would grow at such a pace as to absorb less than the total economic development. N. G. Pierson's 1902 German publication was less optimistic.[21] He wondered if fertility would continue to decline with advances in civilization, and was not ready to dismiss Malthus' dire predictions so casually as Pigou. Brentano held that rising incomes affected fertility indirectly by producing various cultural effects which gave rise to concomitant systems of family limitation. Patten argued in 1895, that as society developed, new pleasures became available which served to satiate primitive appetites and passions, thereby reducing the frequency of sexual union. Hankins wrote an article for the 1930 *Publications of the American Sociological Society* entitled "Does Advancing Civilization Involve a Decline in Natural Fertility?" It reasoned that mental and physical demands upon the individual made by modern society resulted in less importance being attached to the family, leading to lowered fertility and smaller family size.[22]

The majority of writers of the latter nineteenth and early twentieth centuries were more optimistic than early nineteenth-century writers regarding man's ability to control his numbers. "Their optimism had its origin in the spread of contraceptive practices and the decline of birth rates in economically advanced countries, and it was reinforced by the thesis that the birth rate tends to decline with the advance of civilization." [23]

This new point of view toward population was the result of the changing attitude toward the cause of population growth. No longer were man's numbers determined by his agricultural sophistication, rather, his collective size was the end product of the interaction of many obvious and subtle factors which had only to be understood to be controlled. Walter Bagehot tersely summarized this new point of view when he stated that "the causes which determine the increases of mankind are little less than all the causes, outward and inward, which determine human action." [24]

This brief review of man's historical concern with population size and growth has demonstrated that population problems are not a new cause suddenly invented to distract attention from other social problems. From the beginning of civilization man has been concerned with questions related to the understanding and control of human fertility. All social problems are aggravated by rapid and uncontrolled population growth. To be so concerned with some other problem—war, racism, poverty or whatever—that we deny population pressures a place high on the agenda of social concerns is to ensure the ultimate failure of all our efforts.

MODERN POPULATION PERSPECTIVES

During the first quarter of this century some demographers turned their attention to the relationship between the spread and growth of technology and changing demographic patterns. Notice was taken of the apparent decline in the rate of population growth as a society moved from one stage of development to another. The shift from high mortality and high fertility to lower mortality and fertility which has taken place in many countries in association with the spread and development of industrial technology is frequently referred to as the "demographic transition."

The demographic transition theory is part of a larger theory of the unilinear evolution of biological and social phenomena. It holds that certain population changes occur in all societies as they change their level of technology from agricultural to industrial. If we recognize only high and low birth and death rates, there are four possible combinations: (1) High fertility and high mortality. This combination results in very little growth and was the condition under which all societies lived until about 1650. Socially and biologically this is a most inefficient combination, necessitating as it does, a high death rate and maximizing the dangers of pregnancy; (2) High fertility and low mortality. This combination produces rapid growth, and if long continued will so contaminate the environment as to endanger the continuation of life; (3) Low fertility and low mortality. This is a highly efficient combination producing slow and manageable growth along with personal security and freedom from disease; (4) Low fertility and high mortality. This would soon prove fatal to a society and is more a logical combination than a real life condition.

The theory of demographic transition holds that as societies develop industrially, they move from the first combination, or stage, through the second and to the third.

The theory of demographic transition enjoyed a considerable amount of popularity prior to World War II. Thompson,[25] Blacker,[26] and others refined the concept and applied it to the population and industrial patterns of various nations, primarily in the Western world. Prior to World War II, birth rates in the United States and in parts of Western Europe had fallen significantly and consistently for almost a century. But immediately after the war, Western birth rates increased rapidly, and demographers began to look more critically at the transition idea.

Petersen pointed out in 1961 that the theory was too simple, too mechanistic. All of the societies in Stage 3 (low fertility and low mortality) are industrial, but not all industrial societies are sufficiently similar in their population patterns to be classed together.[27] Petersen cites areas of the world to which the transition theory does not apply. Birth rates in both France and the United States were going down when the first demographic data were collected, which was before any great amount of industrialization had occurred. The association between urban residence and lower fertility suggested by the transition theory does not exist in India and some other underdeveloped countries. Petersen says that China does not conform to any of the three demographic types but rather is a distinct new type.[28]

The transition theory overlooks the implications for population growth of the governmental structure and policies of the various industrial societies. The study of industrial, totalitarian societies points up the fact that it makes a real difference how and whether the state intervenes in the processes of fertility, mortality and migration.

Frank Lorimer, writing in his 1954 *Culture and Human Fertility,* says the demographic transition notion is useful for indicating a general tendency but warns that it might convey a false sense of simplicity and uniformity. He argues that there is no necessary relationship between changes in mortality and changes in fertility except that declining mortality creates a condition favorable to declining fertility.[29]

Cowgill, at the conclusion of his 1950 articles on growth cycles, concluded by saying: "No generalizations ascribing identical causes for all population growth cycles are valid." [30] In his 1942 edition of *Population Problems,* Thompson asserted: "The chief factors in population growth in the modern world will be studied in some detail, *on the assumption that there is no natural law of population growth* but rather that the conditions of life, both physical and social, determine this growth and that *it varies from group to group* as these conditions vary." [31]

The mood of demographers has thus changed from one of confidence to one of caution. No longer are predictions of future growth made on the basis of theory derived from studies of past population patterns. The search for "the law" by which population grows has been abandoned. In its place is the realization that population growth results from a sometimes subtle, sometimes obvious interplay of forces; including but not necessarily limited to: (1) the policies and programs of public and private institutions; (2) human psychology and social organization; (3) dietary and nutritional needs.

PRESENT POINTS OF VIEW

Demographers and population analysts are of two points of view today. On the one hand are those who envision a technical solution to the population problem. Biologist Garrett

Hardin defines a technical solution "as one that requires a change only in the techniques of the natural sciences, demanding little or nothing in the way of change in human values or ideas of morality." [32] What most of those who seek a technical solution have in mind is a major breakthrough in agricultural technology. In fact, since 1968, the U.S. Government Agency for International Development (A.I.D.) has expounded on the "Green Revolution" as the panacea for the world's population ills, as if the development of a few new strains of rice and wheat were sufficient. Some of these food fadists like to talk about the fantastic number of people who could be supported by the new agriculture, and they mention populations of three to ten times the present size of the world. They neglect to say, however, why, if this is true, over half of the world's present population is underfed. And it's getting worse, not better.

Those who argue that a greater food production will alleviate population pressures are unbelievably simplistic in their reasoning. "Man does not live by bread alone" is not only a religious principle, but a social reality as well. In fact, those who push the food-people formula actually worsen the problem. By misleading the public and the government to think that more tractors and fertilizer can redeem our world, they lull everyone into a false sense of security, which may, in the end, prove to be the security of the grave. If overnight, enough food were available to feed all the world at an acceptable level, the population problem would still remain. It might even be intensified since hundreds of millions of people, still living in crowded, polluted environments, still without jobs or homes, education or purpose, and with increased energy and expectations, could wreak havoc unimaginable to the present hungry millions. Such a food increase would also accelerate population growth since starvation and malnutrition would no longer take their toll. Stanford biologist John Thomas says, "The problem is *not* can we feed *additional* people, but can we feed the number we now have without ruining the environment so much it cannot support us." [33]

Greater production of food would also aggravate the population problem because it would result in greater density of human populations. The evidence is abundant that man without sufficient privacy becomes mentally and physically sick. For too long, Americans, particularly the intellectual and the religious, have quoted John Donne's lines about no man being an island, entire to himself. But if man is not an island, what is he? Robert Ardrey some years ago wrote a book called the *Territorial Imperative,* in which he argued convincingly that man, and most other living creatures, has an innate and inescapable need to occupy and dominate a sovereign physical space. In this sense at least, man must be an island or he cannot be man.

Other technocrats tell us that our population problem would disappear if we converted to electric cars, mass transportation, multiple-unit dwellings, etc. They write carefully reasoned papers expounding on the benefits to be derived from such changes in our economic and industrial systems. What they apparently do not realize is that these changes are enormously expensive. The funds for such a radical realignment of our relationship to the environment are not, and never will be available because they must be constantly poured back into the existing system to support an ever expanding population.

The second school of thought among demographers today, which I share, holds that there is no technical solution to population problems. The problems themselves are the result of past technical successes.

Can Science Save Us? was the title of a popular book written some 20 years ago.[34] The title was seemingly intended as a rhetorical question to which the answer was obviously *yes.* For this was the attitude of the nineteen-forties and fifties. The supreme arbiter of all questions and the omnipotent legislator of the human condition—this was Science. It promised gadgets galore and solutions supreme. But the last two decades have taught us that science is a servant and technology a tool. They will do whatever they are commanded, but they have no initiative or direction of their own.

Science and technology have created for us at least as many problems as they have solved. This has been true because of our infatuation with technology and, as is the custom in such affairs, we took all she would give, with little thought of the consequences. Robert Oppenheimer, the physicist who helped develop the atomic bomb, commented: "It is my judgment that when you see something that is technically sweet, you go ahead and do it, and you argue about what to do about it only after you have had your technical success."[35] Historian Arnold Toynbee sees technology punishing modern man:

> Man has now decisively overcome Nature by this technology, but the victor has been technology, not Man himself. Man has merely exchanged one master for another, and his new master is more overbearing than his former . . . Nature used to chastise Man with whips, Man's own technology is now chastising Man with scorpions.[36]

Scientists of all fields now realize the need for nonscientists to give directions to their work. In deciding its course of action, science asks only, "Is it possible?" never, "Is it good?" Man makes his own world. Science can help us build a palace or a slum. Which it does will depend upon our political and moral courage in making the hard decisions which our times demand.

Only a commitment of the human will coupled with a "fundamental extension in morality" (Garrett Hardin's phrase) can save us. We must realize, as the philosophers have tried to tell us, that "freedom is the recognition of responsibility" rather than the blind addiction to personal and group interests so widely practiced today.

In a beautiful essay called, "The Tragedy of the Commons," Garrett Hardin points out the inevitable ruin which follows when every individual seeks to maximize his own good. He pictures a common pasture on which all herdsmen graze their cattle. Every herdsman decides for himself how many cattle he should put onto the pasture. Since the costs of overgrazing and replenishing the pasture are borne by all, each individual considers only his personal return when deciding on the size of his herd. Soon all herdsmen have decided to maximize their profits by steadily increasing the number of their cattle. Soon the pasture is incapable of supporting the herd, and the herdsmen, rather than maximizing their return have lost it all. The only salvation for the herdsmen rests in their surrender of the right to add cattle to the herd without restriction.[37]

The mood of many demographers as the world enters the 1970s is grim. So desperate is the world and the national situation that an increasing number of usually placid demographers, biologists and nutritionists have joined with conservation and pollution critics to plead for immediate and drastic action. Georg Borgstrom's *The Hungry Planet*, Paul Ehrlich's *The Population Bomb,* Paul and William Paddock's *Famine 1975!*, Lincoln and Alice Days' *Too Many Americans*, Robert and Leona Rienow's *Moment in the Sun* are but five recent expressions of the climate of crisis rapidly eroding the easy optimism of the technocrats so dominant over the past two decades.

This revival of doomsday demography cannot be dismissed lightly, for those who lead it possess impeccable scientific credentials: Borgstrom is Professor of Food Science at Michigan State University; Ehrlich directs graduate study for the Department of Biological Sciences at Stanford; the Days are demographers associated with Yale University; Paul Paddock is a 21-year veteran of the U.S. Foreign Service serving mostly in undeveloped nations, and his brother William is an experienced agronomist who established several agricultural programs and schools in South America; Robert Rienow is Professor of Political Science at State University of New York at Albany. [His wife Leona, co-author, is a free-lance writer.]

The most widely known of these "prophets of gloom and doom," as critics have called them, is Paul Ehrlich, the Stanford biologist. Books about population problems are usually written by experts whose language cannot be understood by the layman or by reporters whose efforts to "tell it like it is" suffer from a lack of knowledge. Ehrlich's *Population Bomb* suffers from neither of these liabilities. He represents that new breed of scientist whose technical competence has been overlaid with human compassion. His is not the dispirited and pedantic pulp belched forth with such monotonous regularity by the scholarly establishment. Ehrlich is a hard-nosed scientist, but he recognizes, as many scientists apparently do not, that facts do not speak for themselves: they must be interpreted. Rather than copping out, as most scientists do by pleading their neutrality, Ehrlich displays the sort of uncommon courage which may well be our only salvation.

The author's summation of all evidence bearing on the population problem is stated in the prologue:

> The battle to feed all of humanity is over. In the 1970's the world will undergo famines. Hundreds of millions of people are going to starve to death in spite of any crash program embarked upon now.[38]

Those who rely on science to save us will find little comfort in this book, for the author builds a compelling case against any such verdict.

But Ehrlich is not the resigned pessimist one might think. The reader is inescapably drawn to the realization that his book was written to awaken the American people to the gravity of the problem and to prod us to take action.

Those of us who are deeply disturbed by the population peril are called alarmists by our more complacent academic brethren. I sense that this is meant as an accusation of undue fright and insufficient intellect. But I take it to mean that we have accurately surveyed the situation and submitted our report. When danger is imminent, alarm is the only relevant response.

5 The Mythology of Family Planners

It is imperative that we give all our citizens, regardless of income, the right to plan the size of their families . . . However, let me make it perfectly clear that these services are offered on a strictly voluntary basis. No one must ever be forced to practice birth control.

—Senate Bill 2108, May 8, 1969 [1]

No couple should have to produce more children than they want; family planning is a basic human right. Fifty years ago these notions of Margaret Sanger's were revolutionary. Prior to that time, parents had little choice but to accept the unplanned and sometimes unwelcome consequences of their sexual drives. As a nurse in a Brooklyn slum, Mrs. Sanger witnessed the daily misery of women frequently but unwillingly pregnant. She listened to their pleas for help, and watched them die because it was not given. The Comstock Laws and the medical profession conspired, the first by intent, the second by indifference, to deny women the control of their own fertility.

Because she attempted to emancipate women from the bondage of unwanted pregnancies, Margaret Sanger invoked the wrath of government, church and school. Her willingness to accept imprisonment and public disapproval in order to make contraceptives available to women who needed them shall long stand as an example of personal courage and social relevance.

The origin of all family planning agencies in this country today may be traced, directly or indirectly, to the philosophy and programs of Margaret Sanger.

However, times change, and Margaret Sanger's philosophy is today not revolutionary, but reactionary. Family planning has become such a conventional idea, so pursued by powerful and respectable organizations, that we have been blinded to its inadequacy. The proliferation of people since World War II has distorted Margaret Sanger's compassion for individuals into a conspiracy against humanity. So preoccupied have family planners been with individual pregnancies, their prevention and spacing, that they have had too little time or thought for the ominous and astronomical increase in American and World population.

In 1883, the year of Margaret Sanger's birth, world population stood at 1.4 billion and the United States' population at just over 50 million. At her death in 1966, world population had reached 3.4 billion, and that of America exceeded 195 million. Family planners usually claim a high degree of success for their programs, but that success is usually measured in terms of pills distributed, patients seen and speeches made. I would suggest, however, that any program having to do with the prevention of pregnancy is less than successful when measured against the above statistics. Personally, I will count my efforts at teaching, program design and political pressure as a total failure if world population growth is not completely stopped during my lifetime.

The population of the world, now totaling 3.6 billion, is rocketing toward its rendezvous with disaster aboard the good ship "family planning." If its trajectory and velocity are to be altered, we must quickly reverse our uncritical acceptance of "parental rights" and exert the full force of reason.

As our waters become undrinkable, our air poisoned, our resources depleted, our countryside littered, our cities ugly and ungovernable, we are beginning to realize that we can no longer tolerate such massive numbers of people. During Margaret Sanger's lifetime, world population increased more than 240 percent, and U.S. numbers almost quadrupled. Family planners then and now helped resolve individual problems associated with too many children, but they were and are irrelevant to societal problems associated with too many people. In fact, family planners aggravate society's problems by opposing new organizations and ideas designed for population control, such as compulsory birth control and zero population growth. A letter written in 1969 by a national leader of a family planning program to agency personnel across the country accuses those working for zero population growth of "zealotry, hysteria and paranoia." The letter ends with the warning: "With friends like these, we don't need enemies."

In 1934 Margaret Sanger said:

> There can be no justification for violating the right of every married woman to decide when and how often she shall undertake the physical and far-reaching responsibilities of motherhood.[2]

In the 1930s these words expressed an emerging viewpoint, one which recognized the possibilities of a rapidly developing contraceptive technology. These same words today represent an established philosophy and millions of dollars in programs. Rather than attacking a problem as Margaret Sanger did, family planners now use her own words to defend a program, to justify their inability or their unwillingness to anticipate new contraceptive developments and the changes in philosophy and program which must accompany them.

The philosophy of family planners is like D.D.T. Twenty-five years ago, both were important breakthroughs, promising a better and safer life for all. Now both have turned on us, threatening to destroy what they helped to create.

The usual reaction of society when it recognizes the existence of a problem is to pass a law restricting the behavior which produces the problem. When American society some 50 to 100 years ago sought to attack illiteracy and disease, laws were passed requiring school attendance and immunization. Economic insecurity and housing inadequacy were alleviated with social security legislation and building and zoning regulations. For half a century family planners have insisted that parents have the right to the number of children they desire; it is now, therefore, difficult, if not impossible, for them to consider the limitation of family size by law.

U.S. Representative Morris Udall of Arizona wrote a generally excellent population article for the December 1969 *Reader's Digest*. Titled "Standing Room Only on Spaceship Earth," the article argued for a halt to U.S. population growth. After endorsing President Nixon's 1969 proposal for a Commission on Population Growth and the American Future and suggesting that the "Congress and the President declare it the goal of the United States to encourage, by decent, humane and voluntary means, a stabilized U.S. population," Representative Udall added:

> But no government will or should ever undertake to tell people when to have, or not to have children. The solution, if there is one, must come from individuals changing certain basic attitudes.[3]

I suggest that this reluctance even to examine the merits and precedents for legislative population control arises from the historical commitment of organizations concerned with population problems to parental freedom of choice. Margaret Sanger, matriarch of the family planning movement, believed that every child should be wanted, and so dedicated her considerable energies and talents to insuring that every couple could, through application of efficient contraceptive technology, give birth to exactly the number of children they desired.

In 1920—even as late as 1960—this desire to free married couples from physiological accidents was part and parcel of a liberal humanitarianism which sought to deliver the individual from the capriciousness of politics, religion and his own biology. Events of the past ten or fifteen years, however, have rendered this initially liberal doctrine conservative, if not reactionary.

It is untenable to argue that human fertility—a condition fraught with potential for either societal destruction or deliverance—should be governed only by private interest. Since World War II, world society has been engulfed by political and racial turmoil. Automation has assumed the physical tasks for which men were once needed, and cybernation promises to appropriate much of the mental. Ignorance and poverty have erased the minds and crippled the bodies of increasing millions as world population has mushroomed. Unless the births which occur to the hundreds of millions of world families are governed by considerations beyond the immediate and the personal, we shall plunge ever deeper into the jungle of political ineffectualness and racial madness from which only a stable and manageable population size will permit our extrication.

We should have learned by now that a complex and intricate social system composed of multifarious racial, religious and cultural groups cannot maintain itself except by law. The history of labor relations and civil rights offers graphic proof that good intentions, private motivations and emotional rhetoric all eventually give way to Taft-Hartley laws, Supreme Court decisions and Civil Rights acts. In commenting upon current population problems, Colorado State Representative Richard Lamm says:

> Like other new social problems, they probably will have to be solved by law. The development of law, strong enough to be enforced, wise enough to be acceptable, will be the challenge of the new generation of lawyers and law makers.[4]

To justify their opposition to law as a means of population control, family planning organizations have constructed an elaborate mythology to support their belief in the ability of their traditional programs to abort the population explosion. At least seven different but converging myths are contained in the mythology. The first three are explicitly stated in family planning literature; the last four are implicit assumptions which motivate family planning personnel and programs:

1. Parenthood is a right rather than a privilege;
2. The objective is to make every child a wanted child;
3. Individuals are free to choose whatever method of birth control they desire;
4. People see the relationship between their own behavior and the good of their society;
5. People always do what is good for them;
6. Education can solve the population problem;
7. Individual family planning equals national population control.

Mythology has peculiar powers over its believers. So convinced are they of the rightness of their cause, that they are able to dismiss or reinterpret all objective evidence or personal experience which tends to cast doubt upon their faith. Rather than rethinking their assumptions, true believers redouble their efforts. The more the real world is unlike the mythology holds it to be, the greater its power to motivate its adherents. For they see the discrepancy between what is and what ought to be as their personal failure to keep the faith. Through periodic meetings at which they confess their shortcomings and rekindle their enthusiasm, believers perpetuate the mythology, and in the process they build in their own eventual demise. As with all true believers, so with family planners.

There was a time in man's quiet past when mythology was sufficient to sustain him, but no longer. The desperate present demands that we live by reason or we will not live. Mankind is now in the throes of an experiment in which man made himself the subject. The question to be decided is man's intelligence. Is he capable of solving, with his gadgets and his audacity, the many problems confronting him? Can he wrench from a reluctant Nature, the secrets of longer life and greater happiness, or will his medical and industrial successes serve only to overburden and eventually destroy those political, economic and social structures which keep him from anarchy? Man is intelligent, but he may be intelligent enough only to demonstrate his essential stupidity.

Let us see how the mythology of family planners fares when examined.

PARENTHOOD AS A PRIVILEGE

Myth Number One—Parenthood is a right rather than a privilege.

Americans are accustomed to think in terms of rights as being inalienable and unchanging. This is, however, a politically naive view, fashioned from an ignorance of history and an inability to understand societal needs. Rights must have a source; they must be created. There are no natural rights conferred upon man by virtue of his being human. Rights are derived from the law and the law is man-made. Rights are, in the last analysis, simply a recognition of that which is seen as necessary in a certain place at a given time. Laws are not sacred and immutable but practical and dynamic. Their purpose is to enable us to live together at an acceptable level of decency and decorum. But if we are to understand the function of law as a regulator of human conduct, we must first briefly recall the history of civilization.

When men lived in small groups of two to ten families, there were few laws because few were needed. They all agreed on what was good and necessary behavior for their small group. In today's world of giant cities, with their divergent racial, religious, political, educational and cultural groups, however, there is little common consent about proper rules of conduct. So law replaces group consensus as a regulator of behavior, its purpose being to reduce to an absolute minimum the frictions which would otherwise overheat the melting pot.

The history of civilization is the process of translating absolute rights into conditioned privileges. Roman fathers 2,000 years ago had the power of life and death over their children.[5] If they so chose, they could leave a child on a hillside to be stolen by animals or killed by the elements. Likewise, Chinese fathers had the right to trade female children in exchange for some needed household item.[6] Up to the turn of the century, American parents had the right to put children to work rather than to send them to school.

But all this has now changed. Laws have been passed which severely restrict the rights of parents over their own children. Compulsory school attendance laws, health laws, delinquency laws, housing laws—all have translated parental *rights* into *privileges*. The next logical extension of this process is to make it a privilege to *have* children. Such laws would serve not only to defuse the population bomb but also to protect firstborn children against the too prolific reproduction of their parents.

Following a group discussion of the need for control of population size, I received a phone call from a man who had been in attendance. "Could you come out to see my wife and me this afternoon?" he asked. Several hours later the three of us were seated in his living room. He began, "I was born into a miserably poor family of 13 children. I was number 11, and nobody ever had any time for me. I didn't get much education, and now I have to work ten hours a day, seven days a week on an assembly line just to get by." Nodding at his wife, he said, "We couldn't hardly make it if she didn't work. Even with both of us working, we have to farm a little on the side to get by."

The conversation with this couple in their early thirties ended with the husband's emphatic statement: "We have three children, and that's all we're going to have."

Recent studies have shown that one of the most crucial factors associated with the economic status of a family is its size; the larger the family, the more likely it is to be poverty-stricken.[7] The chance of a child's acquiring an education, a healthy body, adequate shelter and a decent job decline as the number of his brother and sisters increases. Approximately

70 percent of all those rejected by Selective Service for reasons of mental deficiency come from families of four or more children. Close to half of the rejectees (47 percent) are from families of six or more.[8]

In today's world, conditions demand that we recognize parenthood as a privilege extended to citizens by the society in which they live. If we continue to insist that parenthood is a right, we shall so inundate our world with people that the very concept of "rights" becomes unintelligible. As Garrett Hardin has written: "The only way we can preserve and nurture other and more precious freedoms is by relinquishing the freedom to breed, and that very soon".[9]

Some will object to defining parenthood as a privilege contending that it smacks of Big Brother and 1984. On the contrary, it would seem that such Orwellian conditions are inevitable *without* such a policy. It is the freedom "to be" rather than the freedom "to have" which is essential to human fulfillment. The more children a couple has, the less freedom they all have to realize the full limit of their potential "to be." If having is elevated in importance over being, those characteristics which we cherish as most human—compassion, courage, conviction—inevitably lose out to our baser instincts: selfishness, ignorance, cowardice. This fact was poignantly captured by a 16-year-old drug addict in Chicago: "You're a fool if you believe what people try to tell you. Everybody is just out for himself. Nobody really cares about anybody else. The way things look for the future, most people would be better off if they never were born." [10]

Complete freedom is anarchy. If freedom may be thought of as the right to swing one's fist, then freedom stops where someone's nose begins. This crude but picturesque analogy serves to illustrate both the relative nature of freedom and its relationship to the population explosion. The more people there are, the less freedom there is.

The essence of man's present predicament was caught by Walter Lippmann, the Dean of American political commentators, in an interview on his eightieth birthday:

> This is not the first time that human affairs have been chaotic and seemed ungovernable. But never before, I think, have the stakes been so high. I am not talking about, nor do I expect, a catastrophe like a nuclear war. What is really pressing upon us is that the number of people who need to be governed and are involved in governing threatens to exceed man's capacity to govern. This furious multiplication of the masses of mankind coincides with the evermore imminent threat that, because we are so ungoverned, we are polluting and destroying the environment in which the human race must live. The supreme question before mankind—to which I shall not live to know the answer—is how men will be able to make themselves willing and able to save themselves.[11]

THE WANTED CHILD

Myth Number Two—The objective is to make every child a wanted child.

The 1967 conference of the International Planned Parenthood Federation proclaimed "the individual's right to plan and limit the family's size . . . to be a basic human right." [12] In 1968, designated as Human Rights year by the United Nations General Assembly, thirty heads of state, representing two-fifths of the human race, presented a resolution to the U.N. urging that "the opportunity to practice family planning be recognized as a basic human right." [13] In May 1969, Senator Joseph Tydings of Maryland introduced a bill in the U.S. Senate entitled "Family Planning: A Basic Human Right." [14] The ultimate purpose of the proclamation, the resolution and the legislation is to ensure that all future children will be wanted rather than accidental. All three naively assume that once it is possible for parents to give birth only when they want to, all family and social problems related to population size will be solved. This assumption was made explicit by a 1969 Planned Parenthood brochure which maintains that Planned Parenthood is working "to reduce the number of unwanted pregnancies and *thus curb excessive population growth.*" (emphasis added).[15] Alan Guttmacher, President of the Planned Parenthood Federation of America writes:

> The underlying philosophy of Planned Parenthood is a very simple one, that is, only to have 'wanted children' born to parents who feel they can be responsible for their upbringing. If this goal is ever realized, it would eliminate many of the social ills which beset us.[16]

But it is entirely possible for every family in America and the world to give birth only to wanted children, yet the population explosion continue or even accelerate. George N. Lindsay, 1968 Board Chairman of Planned Parenthood-World Population, asserted that "it is mainly the more fortunate Americans, confirmed contraceptive users, who are causing U.S. population growth by producing 'wanted babies' so abundantly." [17] A 1966 Gallup Poll indicated that 41 percent of all American women wanted four or more children,[18] a condition which, if realized, would make the baby boom of the forties seem like a lullaby.

Contrary to public opinion it is not the poor who most aggravate the population problem; it is the middle class. Demographer Alice Day says, "By far the major portion of our United States population growth comes from middle and upper middle class families who account for 80% of the children born. If poor families, whose childbearing rate is higher, had had only the same number of children the middle and upper groups did, the total number of children would have been only 4% less." [19] The Committee on Population of the National Academy of Sciences reports that "there seems little doubt that the rise in fertility in the United States is caused more by the preference for larger families among those who consciously choose the number of children they have than by the high fertility in the impoverished segments of the population."[20] In an article called "A Limit to 'Wanted' Babies," *Medical World News* reported in December 1968 that "the main source of population overloading isn't the poor or near poor but the middle class and the rich who produce seven out of ten babies in the U.S. each year." Richard Day, M.D., writing in the *American Journal of the Diseases of Childhood*, traces the population crisis to the fact that so many affluent families who practice birth control nevertheless give birth to three or more children.[21]

By insisting that contraceptives are to be used only to allow parents to have the number of children they want, family planners unnecessarily restrict their efforts to narrowing the gap between anticipated and actual fertility. Seldom do they ask why parents want a certain number of children. For some reason that desire is assumed, at least implicitly, to be immutable. Therefore few programs to change attitudes are undertaken, and family planners give almost all of their attention to improving contraceptive technology and distribution.[22]

Some future historian will look back on the twentieth century and write that in the year 19—, laws were passed in America which struck down forever that anachronistic practice to which we had too long adhered—the right to have as many children as we wanted. That "want" after all is socially created and may be socially redefined. No one is born wanting a certain number of children any more than one wants at birth to speak English or to eat with a fork. The desire to give birth to one, four, seven or fifteen children is thus exposed for what it is—an accident—conditioned by the time and place of our own birth. That future historian will consider us as uncivilized for having permitted unregulated births as we do the Romans and Chinese for their "irresponsible" behavior.

FREEDOM, RESPONSIBILITY AND EDUCATION

Myth Number Three—Individuals are free to choose whatever method of birth control they desire.

Family planning organizations emphasize the fact that they do not force birth control upon anyone. On the contrary, these organizations insist that their mission is to ensure that individuals are free to choose whatever method of birth control they desire. Complete freedom of the individual in deciding to use birth control and in choosing the method; this is the stated operating practice of family planners. A noble-sounding goal, but honored more in its breach than in its application.

In reality family planners do use force on their clients: For one thing, they have, until recently, forced them to be married or to lie about their marital status. As a concession to community values, family planning services have been offered only to the married; little provision was made for the unmarried who might want and need birth control help. In some parts of the country, contraceptives are still denied to the unmarried by law and by custom, while in other places legal barriers have been lowered and operating procedures changed. Still, however, the unmarried do not have equal access to contraceptive advice and technology. Such access is universally recognized by family planners as a basic human right, but this right is generally denied to unmarried minors, especially if they are poor. These girls can usually secure contraceptive assistance only if an unwanted, out-of-wedlock pregnancy first occurs. Yet this is the very right fertility control is supposed to protect.[23]

Family planners also discriminate against men by emphasizing female contraceptives: foams, jellies, diaphragms, IUDs, pills. The Planned Parenthood Association of Greater Kansas City had a total of 4,739 patients during 1969. The Pill was prescribed for 3,770 (79.5%) of these, IUDs for 567 (12%), diaphragms for 102 (2.2%), foams, jellies and creams for 93 (2.0%), rhythm for 5 and condoms, the only male contraceptive listed, was prescribed for a grand total of three patients. The condom, while available through family planning organizations, gets little publicity and relatively little use. Vasectomy, a quick, painless and highly effective surgical technique which renders the male sterile, is neither advertised nor available from family planners, though they do on occasion (and if requested) make referrals.

In reality family planners offer only a limited number of "respectable" contraceptives to their clients.[24] Such things as abortion, sterilization and "unnatural" sexual relations are certainly effective in preventing unwanted pregnancies, but they are defined as "bad" by family planners and their use is not condoned. By imposing their own morality upon their clients, family planners offer mute but eloquent testimony to the fact that they have goals other than the prevention of pregnancy. Access to birth control information and techniques is limited by the conscience of those who operate family planning programs and by that of the religious and governmental officials who support them with words and money. It makes good public relations for family planners to herald themselves as citadels of unrestricted freedoms, but there is a difference between preachment and performance.

Myth Number Four—People see the relationship between their own behavior and the good of their society.

"Social responsibility" is an intriguing concept. It has long been upheld in America by religion and government as a desirable goal for the individual citizen. We are urged to vote, to attend meetings, to pay taxes, to defend our faith and our country, to choose an occupation, to set an example for the young—all in the name of "social responsibility." Certainly a democracy, more than any other form of government, is dependent upon the involvement and the allegiance of its people. However, some decisions and actions of the individual have traditionally not been defined as part of one's social responsibility. Family planners like to believe that social responsibility is a consideration in parenthood, affecting the number of children born to a husband and wife. Not so! Parenthood has so long been thought of as unlike any other condition, that we do not apply the same reasoning to it. With the categorical assertion that "parenthood is private," we make it immune to appeals for reason and responsibility.

But for another reason, also, it is unrealistic to expect individual parents to act in the best interest of society. Our social system is far too intricate and much too large for any individual fully to understand the consequences of his own behavior. In deciding to have another child, the well-to-do couple thinks only of their ability to support the child and their desire for one. They do not think about the fact that their new child will consume five times as much of the world's resources as a baby born in India or an American slum.

There seems to be in operation a "law of universal exclusion" by which individuals convince themselves that they are somehow different from all other human beings, not subject to the same emotions and irrational actions. It is "other" people who litter the countryside with waste thrown from automobiles. In disposing of those bottles along the roadside, "we" were avoiding possible injury to our children resulting from a sudden stop. Our neighbor does not vote because he is indifferent to the problems of government. We did not vote, however, because we were involved on election day with other good causes which kept us from the polls. A friend bought a fancy color television to impress us; we bought the same set because it gets all 84 channels. The family "across the tracks" has a houseful of kids because they don't know any better. We have too many because we love children.

It is difficult for people to see the relationship between their parental behavior and the good of their society, for the societal consequences are neither immediate nor direct. Thus it is impossible for individual parents to realize that they are part of the population problem. Because of their inability to see this relationship, the question of social responsibility involved in parenthood is seldom raised. A recent bumper-sticker announced that, "The Population Bomb is Everybody's Baby," but I daresay the truth of that statement went unnoticed by most of those who saw it and many of those who displayed it.

Myth Number Five—People always do what is good for them.

The very fact that people have problems would seem sufficient to refute this assumption. Hundreds of millions of dollars are spent yearly by Americans on quack medicines, youth elixirs, stimulants, depressants. The more far-fetched the claim for a product, the greater its demand.

Russell Lynes some years ago wrote a book called *The Taste Makers* in which he argued that how we spend our money and our leisure is determined for us by the advertising industry and the mass media.[25] This argument is best caught in the familiar phrase, "What's good for General Motors is good for the country." Somewhat more recently in *The Affluent Society*, John Galbraith contended that the supply of goods today creates its own demand rather than the other way around, as has been true historically.[26]

To contend that people *do* what is good for them assumes that they first *know* what is good for them. So complex and complicated is today's world that no individual can possibly comprehend all the options available in any particular situation. Neither can we anticipate all the possible consequences of our actions. We are like the four blind men trying to describe the elephant by touching different parts of its anatomy. One of the most frustrating characteristics of our age is the competing and often contradictory claims made by products, politicians and pressure groups. We are bombarded by so much information, so poorly integrated, that rather than enlightening and motivating, it tends to obscure and neutralize. Overwhelmed by all those who "tell it like it is," and intimidated by others who urge us to "keep the faith, Baby," the ordinary citizen simply withdraws into the cocoon of noninvolvement, from which we are then impervious to the outside world. We exercise our freedom by choosing to surrender it; we find our personal good at society's expense—a fool's bargain which time and events will unmask!

During 1969 conflicting statements were issued by knowledgeable and responsible individuals concerning the proper course of action to take on the population problem. Scientists meeting at the John Muir Institute in Aspen, Colorado, in September termed voluntary birth control "insanity"[27] and called for some kind of official action to restrict the birth rate.

In December 1969 the President of Planned Parenthood-World Population, testifying before the Senate Committee on Labor and Public Welfare in support of a pending family planning bill, attacked this point of view:

> In the last year, a number of prophets of doom have rushed into the headlines to pronounce the verdict that voluntary fertility control is "insanity." These men have little knowledge of the potential of improved family planning programs and improvements in the delivery of services and techniques. They believe that population growth can be brought under control only through governmental coercion and decree.
>
> I do not share their despair. The appropriate response, in my view, is to mobilize rapidly a total, coordinated U.S. program by government, in collaboration with voluntary health services, in an all-out maximum effort to demonstrate to the world what voluntary fertility control can accomplish in a free society.[28]

It is understandable that the ordinary citizen is confused by such contradictory positions from reputable sources. However, it should be noted that family planning organizations have a vested interest in voluntarism, both because those who use their services choose to do so and because the bulk of their work force is made up of volunteers donating their time. This means that we must somewhat discount the attachment of family planners for voluntarism as an example of their instinct for organizational survival rather than a dispassionate response to society's need. Critics of voluntarism, on the other hand, risk their professional reputations and their future careers by insisting that compulsion is the only adequate response to the population dilemma.

Myth Number Six—Education can solve the population problem.

It has always been said of whatever problem man has faced,

"Education is the answer." But it has never been sufficient. In fact education alone cannot solve even the education problem, and laws are passed to correct deficiencies in the educational process itself. It seems a little naive then to suggest that we rely solely on education to persuade individual parents not to have too many children. Certainly education is necessary in our effort to check population growth, but it is by no means sufficient.

Even though attempts have been made to educate smokers to the dangers of cigarettes, more people are now smoking than in 1964 when the Surgeon General's report linking cigarettes to cancer was issued.[29] Drivers continue to sit on their seat belts despite the educational campaign by the National Safety Council which urges us to "buckle up for safety." A similar fate awaits our well-intentioned efforts to educate for "responsible parenthood." Education is individual; the population explosion is societal. A societal problem cannot be solved by a technique designed for individual development. To say that education can solve the population problem is as unreasonable as saying that crime prevention, labor relations, social security and land use can be sufficiently controlled by education, without recourse to the legislative and judicial processes.

In fact there is a danger in education. It is that we will become so accustomed to discussing a thing, so adept at analyzing and recommending, so fascinated with our verbal facility, so busy with meetings and resolutions, that we never do anything. The *Population Bulletin* published by the Population Reference Bureau characterized population trends in 1969 as "The 'Talk-No Do' Syndrome." The *Bulletin* said:

> The population movement in the United States, the United Nations, the majority of the world's developing nations—is still bogged down in talk . . . If the "Talk-No Do" syndrome of 1969 was merely a phase that any social revolution must pass through, then it was a step forward. But it can easily become a habit, a substitute for getting on with the job.[30]

Those of us who teach are continually disheartened at the difficulties encountered in trying to teach what people do not want to learn. It used to be commonly assumed that education could do away with most if not all of the irrationalities and inconsistencies of the human mind. It was thought that as education increased, hate and prejudice would decline. But it has not turned out to be so. Rather than eliminating prejudice, education has modified its method of expression. No longer so violent or so obvious, it is no less vicious or destructive. To contend that education can do more with the population problem than with the race problem requires a kind of blind faith ill suited to our day.

FAMILY PLANNING AND POPULATION CONTROL

Myth Number Seven—Individual family planning equals national population control.

In his 1967 *Science* article, "Population Policy: Will Current Programs Succeed?" Kingsley Davis points out that America has no policy in regard to population. As director of international population and urban research at the University of California at Berkeley, Davis shows that none of the more than 30 countries now trying to curb population growth seems to have any idea what their goals are. All of them equate individual and voluntary family planning with national population control. But Davis says, "There is no reason to expect that the millions of decisions about family size made by couples in their own interest will automatically control population for the benefit of society. On the contrary, there are good reasons to think they will not do so." [31]

Since current family planning programs have no clear cut and identifiable objectives, any decline in fertility, no matter how short range, is seized upon as justification for the programs. Some point to America's present growth rate of 1.0 percent per year, compared to Africa's 2.4 percent or Latin America's 2.9 percent, as proof that the United States has solved the problem. What is not pointed out, however, is that population growth occurs in waves, and this nation is currently at the foot of an ominous new wave. As the baby boom of the forties and fifties comes of age, the number of births will increase. If we may judge from several recent studies which show an increasing number of third and fourth children suburban families, then we are forced to conclude that not only will the absolute number of births go up, but so will the rate of increase. In fact, the U.S. birth rate rose three-tenths of one percent during the 12-month period ending in September 1969 as compared to the same period in 1967–68.[32]

The year 1969 may have been the beginning of the end for family planning organizations. Despite the fact that the federal government was much more receptive to them than ever before, "many respected authorities in 1969 began to question whether family planning could offer much more than a humane and badly needed help to the tiny minority of American families which are classified as poor or near-poor—that is, whether it could have a major impact on U.S. population growth." [33]

In a controversial *Science* essay, demographer Judith Blake criticized family planning organizations for not attacking the fundamental cause of United States population growth which she defined as the desire of the majority of Americans for families of more than three children. She accused family planners of having goals related only to means of contraception and none having to do with family size.[34]

Planned Parenthood is a service program designed to provide contraceptive assistance to individuals in order to further whatever personal goals they may have. The evidence is abundant that the accomplishment of these individual goals will do little to achieve a manageable rate of population growth. Planned Parenthood of Greater Kansas City, for example, had 2,136 new patients during 1969. Of this total, 566 (38%) already had three or more children and 212 (10%) already had five or more.[35] Regardless of how well the program operates, it is too little, too late when applied to families who already have more children than is consistent with society's welfare.

A related inadequacy of voluntary family planning programs is that not enough people volunteer. Planned Parenthood operates approximately 500 clinics nationwide yet they report serving only 350,000 women (and apparently no men) each year. Of this number 275,000 are poor, yet Planned Parenthood's own estimate puts the number of medically indigent women who want to avoid pregnancy at five million.[36]

At present none of the organizations working in the population field would restrict the number of children parents could have. All of them—from Planned Parenthood to the Association for Voluntary Sterilization and the Campaign to Check the Population Explosion—are committed philosophically to parental freedom of choice. This position was succinctly stated in a letter written to me in 1968 by the Director of a National population organization:

> Neither this organization nor any of the others you have mentioned would support a policy of compulsory birth limitation. It is our view that parents in the United States and overseas must be provided with access to the latest medical information and methods to limit conception, to make a free choice with regard to family size. We can and do argue that smaller families are desirable for a variety of reasons, but we would not join any efforts to devise or impose limits on the family size in the United States or elsewhere.

Aside from a philosophical commitment to parental choice, however, family planners find themselves opposed to legal controls for strategic reasons. In order to gain wider public acceptance, every effort is made to pacify religious and political opposition by repeated insistence that contraceptives are produced and disseminated only so women may have the number of children they want. This unwillingness to evoke opposition undoubtedly has made family planning less controversial than it might have been, but it has thereby been made less effective as a method for the control of population size.

The one organization which has at least discussed restrictions on parenthood is Zero Population Growth, Inc. At its September 1969 board meeting, Z.P.G. passed the following resolutions, the intent of which was to encourage governmental action to restrict the number of children born to individual parents:

1. It is resolved that parenthood is not an inherent right of individuals but a privilege extended by the society in which they live. Accordingly, society has both the right and the duty to limit population when either its physical existence or its quality of life is threatened.

2. We further resolve that every American family is entitled to give birth to children, but no family has the right to have more than two children.

3. We further resolve that the Congress of the United States must (a) enact legislation guaranteeing the right of parenthood to all Americans but restricting the number of natural (not adoptive) children to two, and (b) adopt and finance a "crash" program to develop a birth control technology sufficient to accomplish this objective without using criminal sanctions.[37]

At its April 1970 Board of Directors meeting, Z.P.G. passed another resolution having to do with family size. This one was directed to parents:

> Z.P.G. recognizes that even if an average family size of two children were instituted immediately and maintained in the U.S., population would continue to grow until after 2000 A.D.; and that the only way to achieve faster population stabilization would be

> to bring down average family size below two natural children. Therefore, the Board of Directors urges all Americans to limit their children to a maximum of two natural children.

As a charter member of Z.P.G. and as a member of the Executive Committee of the national board, I introduced the first three resolutions described above, and they were adopted after considerable discussion. Since their passage, however, Z.P.G. has backed away from any hint of compulsory birth control. Many of our directors and members believe that our political effectiveness would quickly disappear if we were to endorse compulsion. They may be right. Senator Joseph Tydings, speaking at the First National Congress on Optimum Population and Environment argued that "strong resistance still exists in Congress to programs promoting voluntary family planning, much less compulsory population control. Indeed, at this time, talk of compulsion constitutes the greatest threat to the success of the voluntary population stabilization movement."

I respect the Senator's judgment of Congressional attitudes toward population programs. But history has demonstrated that there is often a distinct difference between the politically attractive and the socially necessary. The popularity of an idea at a point in time is more a reflection of public opinion than of human need. And those opinions change as the needs become more apparent.

Perhaps the biggest reason for compulsory birth control being politically unattractive at present is that no one has carefully examined the need and the precedents for it. Nor has it been shown to be directly related to the very survival, much less the welfare, of all the human race. Jumping to conclusions has always been a favorite recreational pastime of Americans. Accordingly, we have always concluded that only a racist or a eugenicist would recommend compulsory birth control. That is patently ridiculous. It's like saying that only a dictatorship would deny people the right to die.

"Don't confuse me with the facts, my mind is made up," so heralded a popular little saying of several years back. Intended to be humorous, it may well have been prophetic.

In March 1968, I received a letter from the director of a Planned Parenthood office in a major American city. The letter said in part:

> I read your paper about the government limiting births with great interest. I think you are right, but I hope that you are wrong. The great fear that has kept the government from getting into the field of family planning has been the thought of compulsory limitations of births. Even to me, an old hand at this game, I dislike the idea of compulsory limitation. At the present rate of growth something will have to be done. This might be the last generation where free choice will be possible.

Old myths cannot cope with new realities. Those who think otherwise simply compound society's problems and intensify their personal frustrations.

Sleep well, family planners, for you live in a dream world, and awake in a madhouse of your own design.

6 Birth Control as Preventive Medicine

Furthermore, it was recognized that the state on occasion would have to exercise compulsion in the best interests of both the community and the individual, specifically in instances involving restraint of vagrants, isolation of mental cases, removal of children from unfit parents, compulsory vaccination, regulation of child labor, and compulsory schooling.

—The Field of Social Work[1]

Medical science today promises that life expectancy may soon be prolonged to 85 and perhaps 100 years. Some of the bolder medical magicians are even suggesting that death may soon be a preventable disease. Indeed such a proposition does not seem entirely beyond reason when we consider the implications of the heart transplant technology and the extra 20 years already added to the average life since 1900.

In the last 100 years, Western medicine has practically eliminated smallpox, diphtheria, scarlet fever, polio and other mass killers. In America almost all children are now innoculated against disease—in effect life is imposed upon many who, if natural selection were allowed to operate, would not survive childhood. And when old age comes, every medical technique available is marshalled to maintain life beyond the point at which death would "naturally" occur.

The technology of death control has developed rapidly over

the past century because government and medicine have deemed it good that man should live long. Governments have supported and rewarded research designed to control death, and medicine has responded as Merlin might have to King Arthur. So preoccupied with death control have government, medicine and the biological sciences become that critics label this trinity, the Health Syndicate. Over the years its awesome efficiency has been exceeded only by the public adulation and reward heaped upon its practitioners. By contrast, those concerned with birth control have been restricted by the law and lampooned by the press.

For example, note these two Associated Press news releases carried only a few months apart:

SPANISH HONOR TO U.S. HEART SURGEONS

Houston (AP)—Dr. Denton A. Cooley and an associate have received the Grand Cross of Alfonso X the Wise from the Spanish government for scientific achievement in heart surgery.

Cooley and Dr. Domingo Liotta were presented Spain's highest scientific award by Dr. Cristobal Martinez-Bordiu, a heart surgeon and a son-in-law of Generalissimo Francisco Franco.

"We honor these surgeons with deep feelings of friendship for their exchange of scientific programs," Martinez-Bordiu said in ceremonies at St. Luke's Episcopal Hospital.

BIRTH CONTROL DEVICES "INDECENT"

Ashland, Wis. (AP)—A birth control crusader, William E. Baird, was arraigned yesterday on a charge of displaying contraceptive devices, termed "indecent articles" under Wisconsin law, in a speech at Northland College last month.

> Baird, director of the Parent's Aid Society of New York, entered no plea, and Judge Walter H. Kate adjourned the case until March 2.
>
> A group of students from colleges in Ripon, Oshkosh, Appleton and Ashland picketed the courthouse during the appearance, carrying signs that read, "Every child has a right to be loved and wanted" and "Ignorance Breeds."

As the technology of death control was perfected, a philosophy concerning its use was also developed. That philosophy held that it was the duty of government to insure that all its citizens shared in these medical miracles. This was accomplished in a simple, straightforward manner—death control was made compulsory. Thus we are not allowed to choose whether we shall be inoculated against disease; for our own and our community's well-being, we are forced to protect ourselves against epidemic and accident. Neither may we choose to die so long as the doctor or a drug can prolong life.

Personally, I want to die with dignity while I'm still active and alert, before I become a parasitic vegetable existing only to document the efficiency of modern medicine, serving only to drain the financial and spiritual resources of my loved ones. Few people, however, see compulsory death control as an abridgement of their freedom because most want to live as long as possible.

In early 1970 the Religious News Service carried a story about Dr. Leslie D. Weatherhead, a famous (and elderly) British minister who publicly claimed that he should have the right to die. "After all," he declared, "Christ chose to die ('No one taketh it from me. I lay it down of myself'). We also, on a humbler plane and with a different motive, should claim the right to die."

Dr. Weatherhead summed up his feelings by observing that "The town in which I live contains many who long to die and I feel our great-grandchildren will express astonishment that with such simple means in our hands we forced people to go on living—if that is a meaningful word—in a condition which if enforced on an animal would lead to a prosecution for cruelty."

John Reeves was a big man, strong as a bull, with a face that reflected neither joy nor sorrow but simply an imponderable determination to meet and master life on his own terms. Big John was past seventy-five when he climbed down from a roof for the last time, to be a carpenter no more. At eighty, his hearing gone and his eyesight fading, he parked his car in his front yard and placed a "For Sale" sign on it. Death was approaching and he was making ready.

But Medicine would not let John die. Now at eighty-five, senility has crippled his mind, he vomits his food and cries softly as he sits. Big John died five years ago, but they will not hold his funeral until Medicine has finished with his body.

It does not seem likely that we Americans will repeal our programs of compulsory death control. That being the case we have no alternative but to balance the birth-death formula by the same process—namely, compulsory birth control. It should be clear to all that compulsory birth control follows compulsory death control as naturally and necessarily as life precedes death. It defies reason to contend that man can manipulate nature at one end of life's continuum without corresponding adjustment at the other end. Once we have intervened in our biological processes, only the most complete control of which we are capable can regain the necessary balance.

We live in a finite world. Whatever the number of people it is capable of supporting, there is a limit. We do know that our world is doing a pretty poor job of supporting its present population of around three and a half billion. How long can we expect to continue to double world population every 35 years? To what end? In what ways will we be better off with seven billion people than with three and a half billion? What possible advantages are there in even minimal population growth? Scores of disadvantages come readily to mind, but not a single benefit. The stork is not the bird of paradise.

With a current population in excess of 200 million, America

does not need any more people. Already we have too few jobs, schools, hospitals and homes. The countryside is being gobbled up at the rate of 40 acres per mile of freeway, and still the journey to work takes longer than it did 100 years ago. The northeastern seaboard has become a vast and confusing megalopolis with up to 100,000 people per square mile. So contaminated is much of our air that a sudden inversion of the wind pattern could choke the life out of thousands of people; indeed such a horror has stricken London twice since 1950. An effective and enforced population policy is the only alternative to national and global suicide.

Just as America has laws compelling death control so we must have laws requiring birth control, the purpose being to ensure a zero rate of population increase. We must come to see that it is the duty of the government to protect women against pregnancy as it protects them against job discrimination and smallpox. And for the same reason: the public good. No longer can we tolerate the doctrinaire position that the number of children a couple has is a strictly private decision carrying no social consequences. There is ample precedent for legislation limiting family size; for example, the law which limits a married person to only one spouse. State laws on bigamy are such that anyone who is married to more than one person at a time is guilty of a felony and is subject to prosecution and imprisonment. Similar legislation restricting the number of children permissible to a couple is more than a possibility; it is an absolute, guaranteed, inescapable reality which shall soon overwhelm us—unless we can quickly devise other ways of looking at the question of population control.

Our present ostrich policy, if long continued, will do us in. Our national leaders are, and have been, singularly unimaginative in their approach to the population problem. They accept the pronouncements of demographers as if they come directly from God. When the demographer announces that the United States population in the year 2000 will exceed 300 million, the politician doesn't ask how such a massive and unmanageable increase can be prevented. Rather he wants to know what must be done to accommodate it. President Nixon has said that America must build a new city of 250,000 every 30 days for the next 30 years, apparently indicating that the federal government, rather than attempting to defuse this demographic dynamite, is content to muffle the explosion.

If it were announced today that America would be invaded in 30 years by 100 million soldiers of a foreign power, the Defense Department would immediately pour hundreds of billions of dollars into new defensive weapons. Laws would be passed to restrict present freedoms, diplomatic efforts would be made to prevent the impending war, and propaganda would be mounted to prepare Americans for the invasion. The demographer's pronouncement evokes no such response, but that is exactly what he is saying.

If we apply the analogy of criminal law to the population problem, we would enact legislation to punish those giving birth to more than the agreed-upon number of children. However, this is a most inefficient and unimaginative approach to the problem. But such has been the usual American method of handling its social problems.

For most of our history, our approach to problems of poverty, crime, education, broken homes, alcoholism, etc. has been remedial rather than preventive. It was an after-the-fact reaction, hastily made and always inadequate. The Great Depression of the thirties demonstrated the intellectual bankruptcy of our social policies, and the New Deal was born. Essentially this was nothing more than the anticipation of future needs and the creation of policies and programs to meet them.

Prior to the Depression, poverty was looked upon more as an individual problem rather than a social problem. If a man were poor, it was due to his personal inadequacy in ability or ambition. "Anyone can get a job who wants one," was an even more popular myth then than now. Accordingly, no poverty prevention programs existed. But the mass unemployment and widespread poverty of the thirties purged our political philosophy of its simplistic notions regarding the causes and consequences of poverty. We finally realized that the structure of the economy was at least, if not more, important than the ambition of the individual. Poverty prevention became the goal and legislative manipulation of the economy, the means.

Prevention must also be our goal in regard to population problems. As with poverty in the thirties, many Americans view birth as due to individual ability and ambition. But the social structure of America with its disdain of the unmarried adult and its maudlin sympathy for the childless couple, fuels the population explosion. "Mother-of-the-year" awards are given only to women who have amply demonstrated their breeding potential. The first American Mother-of-the-Year award was presented to a Mrs. Johnson in 1935. At the age of 59, Mrs. Johnson had 6 children and 13 grandchildren.[2] Mrs. Smith won the 1936 motherhood medal. *The New York Times* described her: "Mrs. Smith loves cooking but does not smoke, drink or sing. Mrs. Smith would like to have had 12 children but thinks her six is pretty good." [3] Immediately below a story on the 1937 Mother-of-the-Year, who was from Nebraska, the same newspaper ran a short news article called, "Other Nebraska Products." [4]

The scoring system for such awards is reminiscent of baseball's yearly batting title which goes to the player with the greatest number of hits in the least number of tries. Less productive mothers (and ball players) perform their task in relative obscurity, feeling somewhat inadequate, but knowing that they too may make the big time if they put out sufficient effort.

A high birth rate is also the result of many of our social policies. Tax exemptions for children, tax credits for homeowners, maternity leaves, and so forth, all reflect a pro-natalist attitude on the part of government. All are remnants of a time long past when America needed more people. The need has been satisfied, but the policies remain.

The history of Mother's Day is interesting in this regard. It was in 1934 that President Franklin D. Roosevelt, acting on a Resolution passed by the Senate, proclaimed Mother's Day as an official American observance. It so happened that during the 1930s the American birth rate was falling at such a rate that politicians and short-sighted demographers were concerned that our population would decline rapidly in size. Following the designation of Mother's Day, motherhood awards grew like Topsy all across the country. The Golden Rule Foundation chose the American Mother-of-the-Year. The American War Mothers, the Catholics, the Baptists, states and cities, fraternal and civic organizations—all elevated motherhood to an officially rewarded status. The birth rate went up. Obviously, it was not Mother's Day which was solely responsible for the fertility increase, but it undoubtedly played a part.

The population explosion of the seventies is a far greater threat to our survival than was the Depression of the thirties. A demographic New Deal is our only hope of salvation. We must acknowledge the health hazards of pregnancy. I am not referring to the dangers which the individual mother runs, but to the infinitely greater threat to the health and welfare of society. I suggest, with tongue only slightly in cheek, that we Americans already define pregnancy as a social sickness. Do we not insist that condom dispensers carry the announcement, "Sold only for the prevention of disease"? Our country and our world is presently engulfed by a pregnancy epidemic which threatens to destroy us all. Public health and safety is now in as much danger from the pregnancy epidemic as it was from smallpox in the eighteenth century, and the solution is the same: the development of effective immunization and the enactment of compulsory legislation. If we will apply public health analogies to the prevention of pregnancy, we will find that it is not all difficult to lay out a sensible and workable program for the solution of population problems.

PUBLIC HEALTH IN AMERICA

Some attempts were made to control epidemic diseases in Colonial times. But not until about 1870 were serious and continuous efforts made to control communicable diseases. Most public health legislation and programs resulted from epidemics which swept the country, killing and maiming thousands of Americans.

Countless epidemics ravaged America between 1800 and 1850—smallpox, yellow fever, typhoid fever, scarlet fever, measles, etc. Isolation and quarantine regulations for smallpox were first passed in 1701. The first smallpox inoculation was given in 1721, but it was not widely used until Jenner's cowpox vaccine was developed and used in Cambridge, Massachusetts, in 1800.[5]

An act authorizing the first local Boards of Health was passed in 1797, and control of communicable diseases became a major function of these local boards about 1870. The American Public Health Association was formed in 1872.

From 1875 to 1925 the control of communicable diseases made great progress. Typhoid, tuberculosis, malaria, diphtheria and smallpox all declined rapidly. Before 1900 tuberculosis was considered such a private disease that no records were kept and it was not reported. "Tuberculosis began to be recognized as a communicable disease and not a family taint, and was made reportable by health departments about 1895."[6] Compulsory pasteurization of milk was introduced in Chicago in 1908 and was intended as a public health measure. The first School of Public Health was formed in 1913 at Harvard and M.I.T.

Even though millions of people were victimized by epidemics and few families escaped the sudden and untimely death of loved ones, medical efforts to control epidemics met with great opposition. Even the threat of death and disfigurement, it seemed, could not break the hold of custom without a struggle. Vaccination and quarantine regulations were resisted by earlier Americans. Only when diseases got completely out of hand, threatening to end all life, could our ancestors break with their past and adopt new medicines and new laws. Fluoridation of water more recently has aroused passions and prejudices, though it had no objective more sinister than the preservation of public health.

One rationale for opposing fluoridation was stated in a 1964 publication:

> If it had been proven, by generations of careful research, that sodium fluoride in water improves the dental health of all children and harms no one, it would still be wrong to fluoridate public water systems, even though a majority of the people voted to do it, because it is compulsory mass medication.[7]

Besides denying the basic concept of democracy—the right of a majority to vote a thing into existence—this point of view rejects fluoridation simply because it is compulsory. I wonder if the author of this statement believes in the right to have smallpox?

Over the years the concept of Public Health has come to include the right of health officers to isolate and quarantine those who have contagious diseases. The individual's freedom to move about has been made secondary to society's right to remain free from contamination. Compulsory treatments and vaccinations have also been enacted as public health measures, and their legality has been upheld by the courts. Physicians are required by law to treat the eyes of infants with a prophylactic (a medicine that protects against disease) and parents are compelled to offer their children for vaccination against smallpox and other contagious diseases. *Corpus Juris Secundum,* which summarizes American law and its judicial interpretation says:

> The liberty of a person is not unconstitutionally invaded by a statute or ordinance denying pupils the right to attend schools unless vaccinated for smallpox, where there is smallpox in the community, or even by an outright compulsory vaccination statute subjecting a person to fine or imprisonment for neglecting or refusing to submit to vaccination. Like-

> wise, due process is not denied by a statute relating to compulsory isolation and hospitalization of tubercular persons. . . .[8]

Despite the fact that these measures are essential for group survival, there are those who label them as communistic, atheistic, fascistic, etc. They profess to see some nefarious intent behind such legislation. Like Chicken Little, they misrepresent the case. What a pity that so many of those with the energy and enthusiasm to get involved with social issues simply compound the problems. While the right-wingers and the religious zealots attack sex education, population pressures build. Consider the plot seen by one minister to destroy America through sex education in the schools:

> It should be evident that the sex educators are in league with sexologists—who represent every shade of muddy gray morality, ministers colored athestic pink, and camp followers of every persuasion—offbeat psychiatrists to ruthless publishers of pornography [*sic.*]. The enemy is formidable at first glance, but becomes awesomely powerful when we discover the interlocking directorates and working relationship of national organizations which provide havens for these degenerates.[9]

As black militants cry genocide, their survival and ours becomes ever more uncertain. They charge that white doctors are using black women as guinea pigs in experimenting with new drugs. The Black Muslim newspaper, *Muhammad Speaks,* for January 23, 1970 describes a 22-year-old black mother who was supposedly given an experimental birth control drug when she was four months' pregnant and died as a result of it. This type of experimentation is said to be common among white doctors who receive a kickback from drugs tested in this manner.

This charge betrays a complete lack of knowledge of the

Food and Drug Administration's very careful supervision of contraceptive usage (see Chapter 8). It also overlooks the fact that medical doctors are required by law and by centuries of tradition to place the welfare of the individual patient above every other consideration. A third error involved in this charge is the fact that black women, and poor women in general, have traditionally not had even the access to contraceptives which they wanted and needed.

Those who raise false issues and oppose legislation which compels us to act in society's best interest, simply do not understand the relationship between society and the individual. They have not made the bargain which civilization demands. They carry in their heads the romantic illusion that they can be their own man (or woman) unfettered by responsibility, ungoverned by any power other than their own wishes. They are, in short, anarchists who long for a state of nature in which every man is his own king. But I suspect that they would be unwilling to surrender their homes, cars, clothes, food, entertainment and other amenities which society furnishes them. Like the child, they want the protection of their parents but dislike being told what to do.

Ideally, society and the individual enjoy a mutual relationship. For protection and life's necessities, the individual agrees, either directly through the ballot, or indirectly by using what society offers, to elevate societal good above individual wishes.

Societal good now demands control of population. "Accidents cause people" is a homely little phrase often voiced by partners in unplanned parenthood. Though usually spoken in jest, the phrase points up how spontaneous and potentially dangerous conception really is. Public ill-health is the result of such accidents. A former President of Colombia, South America, describes it graphically:

> I have visited the poorest slums of the republic and recommend the same visit to the people who examine the population problem above all from the moral point of view. What can we say of the fre-

> quent incest; of the terrible proliferation of prostitution of children of both sexes; of frequent abortion; of almost animal union because of alcoholic excesses?
>
> It is, in consequence, impossible for me to sit back and examine the morality or immorality of contraceptive practices without thinking at the same time of the immoral and frequently criminal conditions that the simple act of conception can produce in the course of time.[10]

In discussing smallpox treatment in 1940, Wilson Smillie, former Professor of Public Health and Preventive Medicine at Cornell University Medical College, wrote: "An ideal program for the complete protection of the community is compulsory vaccination of all children before the first birthday, with revaccination required before the child enters school." [11]

I recommend that we approach the control of pregnancy in exactly the same way. Assuming that we soon could have a vaccine to immunize against fertility, it would then be possible to inoculate all children. Unlike the smallpox vaccine which furnishes lifelong protection, however, the anti-fertility vaccine will have to be reversible. Following marriage, fertility could be temporarily restored by another shot. After the permitted number of births, permanent immunity to fertility could be re-established.

This fertility immunization should not be for women only. For two reasons, both male and female fertility should be prevented. First because it is medically unwise to place the entire burden of pregnancy prevention on the woman. If we push the public health analogy a little further, we can identify the female as the carrier of the pregnancy disease; but the male is the agent which activates her dormant condition. Pregnancy is endemic in the female, but it assumes epidemic proportions only in association with the male. Therefore, the disease could be much more effectively controlled if both male and female were inoculated. If both partners in potential conception have been immunized against fertility, the odds are much better that conception will not occur.

A second reason for immunizing both male and female has to do with its political acceptability. To inoculate only one sex smacks of discrimination and would immediately arouse the opposition of half the population. Because the female reproductive process is better understood and her participation more obvious, any single-sex immunization would undoubtedly be directed at the woman. Militant feminists would immediately denounce any such female-oriented program as unjust. And they would be right. During Senate hearings on the oral contraceptive in late 1969, women demonstrators in various cities carried signs announcing: "Women Poisoned for Men's Benefit," "Men—You Try the Pill," "Make the Men Worry," "Women's Rights—Male Pregnancy."

One reason for the female reproductive process being better understood is simply because it has been studied more. The overwhelming majority of medical doctors in America are, and have been, men. I suspect that it is more than coincidence that female sexual anatomy and physiology have been so thoroughly studied by male doctors. Just as black militants accuse white social scientists of studying Negro social problems while ignoring those of whites, so militant feminists criticize the male-dominated medical profession for its preoccupation with female medical problems. One woman charged: "They're still dirty-minded little boys who like to feel and gawk at some naked female. But now their victims have to pay them instead of having them arrested."

If America is to define birth control as preventive medicine the technology is only half the battle. Obviously, no program such as I have described can possibly be enacted until our contraceptive technology is much more sophisticated than at present. This sophistication is likely to come, however, only if aroused public opinion demands it. When all of us realize the imminent threat to our lives and homes from uncontrolled pregnancy and demand protection—only then will our "leaders" follow. Our present official neglect and public apathy toward population control are crimes against humanity, and we will not escape the punishment.

Our nation in the sixties witnessed what can happen when we commit ourselves to an objective. Billions of dollars and the best minds in the country got us to the moon in less than a decade. Many of us now wonder if it was worth the trip. But the point is, we did it because we committed ourselves to it. That same commitment to the salvation of our own planet is now called for, and it must begin with population control.

Some biologists and ecologists are calling for the treatment of water supplies with chemicals which inhibit fertility. Others recommend that the entire country be sprayed with a chemical which induces sterility. Such programs would not be very efficient, for they would disturb the fertility of the animal and vegetable life on which men depends for food and fibre. The fact that these suggestions are being made by reputable scientists, however, is graphic proof that those most familiar with our predicament realize the need for immediate and drastic action.

Ideally, democracy is that system of government which allows for the full and free participation of all its citizens in the decision-making process. Democracy assumes that all those who take part are aware of the alternatives and consequences for any given decision. It further assumes that all parties to the decision can recognize and act upon the common good rather than vested interest. If this ideal were a workable reality, we could feel some confidence that democracy can come to grips with population control.

The available evidence, however, leads to the unhappy conclusion that democracy may not be equipped to make the hard decisions now demanded. Some years ago Eric Fromm, the German psychoanalyst, wrote a book called *Escape from Freedom*.[12] He argued that freedom becomes an intolerable burden for people. It demands too much of us by way of keeping informed and involved. Freedom makes us responsible for our own condition, and if that condition is not to our liking, we have only ourselves to blame. Freedom requires that people see issues clearly and act decisively. But most of us cannot commit ourselves to the lifelong exercise of freedom with its frustrations and anxieties. Like Don Quixote we make periodic forays against an assumed enemy, but we soon retire, leaving the battle in progress and out of control. With reference to public health, Smillie makes the point that "compulsory vaccination, which has proved time and again to be a simple, but perfectly effective, procedure in preventing smallpox in any community is losing ground. Its enforcement meets with constant opposition from the general public for a variety of reasons: most important of which is that a regulation enforcing compulsory vaccination is an infringement on personal liberty." [13] Freedom may yet be the death of us.

This is why some scientists and citizens concerned with population control recommend the unannounced and unauthorized use of fertility inhibitors. Remembering the widespread and prolonged opposition to the fluoridation of public water supplies in the 1950s and early 1960s, the prospect for agreement on preventive birth control is not good.

For my part, I would like to preserve democracy. Even more, however, I want to preserve the human race. If both can be accomplished we will be extremely fortunate. But if only one can be achieved, humanity takes precedence over democracy. Survival of the human species is man's fundamental obligation to life. All else is secondary. It's up to us. If Americans of all races, religions, classes and creeds can immediately act to make the control of population growth our Number One national priority, both democracy and humanity can be rescued. Otherwise, democracy is a luxury we can no longer afford. If, as a people, we cannot make the decisions necessary for survival, then those decisions will have to be made for us.

For our own good, compulsory birth control must be implemented. If only we can recognize how necessary compulsion is to our society; it is not something dreamed up by the 1984 designers of the Brave New World. Compulsion has long been at home among civilized men. Perhaps it will help to demonstrate that fact.

RIGHTS AND PRIVILEGES

"Do your own thing." "Tell it like it is." These were two of the cardinal doctrines of the late sixties and early seventies. Both assumed complete freedom, not to mention infinite knowledge and awesome power of the individual. It was as if society had reverted to the state-of-nature idea so popular in the time of Rousseau, whereby every man was his own rule-maker and no man need consider the wishes or welfare of his neighbor. As a reaction against growing impersonality, institutional rigidity and bureaucratic irresponsibility, these modern doctrines are understandable and healthy, both for the individual and for society. If they become long-term operating philosophies, however, as might well happen, they can only produce chaos. Imagine what would happen to America if no one felt compelled to abide by any of the several hundred thousand laws devised to protect us from each other. The following is a partial listing of some of the diverse powers which American law invests in the government:[14]

1. regulate the custody of minor children
2. exercise eminent domain
3. provide for location, construction and repair of highways
4. require compulsory dipping of cattle to prevent tick infection
5. regulate the use of public lands by sheep and cattle
6. pass oil inspection laws
7. prescribe qualifications for public office holders

8. require that veterans be given preference in appointments to office
9. regulate the salary of public officers and employees
10. require teachers to show that they do not have a communicable disease
11. provide and regulate education
12. exclude children from school if they have not been vaccinated
13. forbid secret fraternities in public schools
14. regulate liability for libel
15. prohibit wasteful use of natural gas
16. regulate use of soft coal by factories near cities
17. regulate insurance payments
18. regulate or prohibit importation of diseased animals

With respect to the rights of parents over their children, American law is explicit:

> The state has an interest in the welfare of children and the authority to protect them which goes beyond the natural right and authority of the parent to the child's custody, since the primary or paramount control and custody of children is with the state, standing in the relation of *parens patrix*. In such capacity, the state may, in a proper case assume the direction, control, and custody of the child, and, accordingly, a parent's rights in respect of the care and custody of his minor children are subject to control and regulation by the state by appropriate legislative or judicial action, and such rights of a parent may be enlarged, restrained, and limited as wisdom or policy may dictate. . . .[15]

We have come a long way from the absolute rights which ancient Roman and Chinese fathers exercised over their children. A Roman father could lawfully take the life of his son even though the son were a Roman Senator. Chinese parents could put a newborn infant to death if its living threatened to overburden the family's resources.[16] American parents have no such far-reaching rights. Even though the parent is a fit and proper person, the rights of American parenthood are not absolute, being subject as they are to governmental control and intervention.

Compulsory Insurance One of the chronic problems of civilized men is the uncertainty of employment. Through accident to himself or technological change in his work, a man may find himself without an income. To offset the individual and social disruption stemming from this loss of earnings, the United States Congress enacted the Social Security program in 1935. Under the terms of this act, a percentage of each worker's salary is set aside for his use after retirement or by his dependents in case of his death. The worker's contribution is matched by the employer and both sums are credited to the worker's account. And all this is compulsory. Employers and employees are forced by law to participate in this savings plan.

Prior to the Depression of the thirties, attempts had been made to encourage people to save. Warnings were issued about the dangers of unemployment and dependent old age. Incentives were designed to entice people to save their money. Some far-sighted souls, seeing the lack of effect from such policies, suggested that individual workers should be forced to save a portion of their income against the time when they would have none. Employers contended that a compulsory clause "will eliminate freedom of choice." Workers held that such an action "will deprive us of money which is rightfully ours." For these same reasons some states continued to carry an elective clause in their legislation even after the courts ruled that compulsory clauses were constitutional.

Whether social security insurance should be elective or compulsory was a nice debating society topic for an afternoon meeting until economic reality made the question irrelevant. What it "should be" became less important than what it "had to be." Compulsory social insurance did not originate in the 1930s, however. England's Daniel Defoe advocated such a plan in the year 1698. A bill for this purpose was introduced in the House of Commons in 1787, but no action was taken. Austria became the first nation to enact a compulsory insurance program in 1851; Germany followed suit in 1884.[17]

In this country, Maryland in 1902 was the first state to enact a compulsory insurance program. The court declared the law to be unconstitutional, however, because it "deprived the worker of his common law rights to sue the employer as guaranteed by the Constitution." [18] Under Theodore Roosevelt's administration in 1908, Congress passed the first workmen's compensation law (containing a compulsory clause) which withstood the constitutional attack. Between 1910 and 1915, 30 states followed suit.[19]

By 1935 the economic plight of Americans was so serious that the last vestige of opposition to compulsory insurance was swept aside. In 1937 the Supreme Court of the United States upheld the constitutionality of the Social Security Act against charges that it was arbitrary, not uniform and usurped the powers of the state. Judge Cardoza delivered the Court's opinion and said in part: "Nor is the concept of the general welfare static. Needs that were narrow or parochial a century ago may be interwoven in our day with well-being of the nation. What is critical or urgent changes with the times." [20]

Richard Lamm, a lawyer and an elected public official, makes the same point with reference to current population problems. He says "any lawyer with a sense of history recognizes that if the time ever comes when this country's survival or even welfare demands restrictions on fertility, the 'felt necessities' will outweigh 'precedent.' " [21]

Despite its central role in protecting American families against economic disaster, Social Security is even today bitterly opposed by some. One such opponent argues that Social Security "is an intellectual fraud, a corruption of the King's English for obviously delusive purposes, and an outright confidence device . . . used to broadcast the myth among taxpayers supporting the system that Uncle Sam, alias Santa Claus, will amply and adequately take care of all Americans on retirement or death." [22]

Fortunately such socially irresponsible opposition has not prevailed. Else we should all still be victimized by economic and medical conditions over which we have no control.

Laissez-Faire The American economy was originally designed to operate according to the doctrine of "Laissez-Faire"—governmental nonintervention. "That government is best which governs least" was the popular idiom by which this principle found expression. Pure and perfect competition was to govern supply and demand, thereby establishing perpetual equilibrium in the market place. By the 1880s this system of free enterprise had produced the robber barons, gigantic monopolies, inhuman working conditions, illegal fortunes and widespread poverty. Thereupon the government abandoned its hands-off policy and the Congress in 1890 enacted the Sherman Anti-Trust Act, one of the first in a long line of legislation designed to control the economy. Since that time, laws have been passed outlawing price fixing, forcing large companies to divest themselves of their holdings, and compelling employers to recognize and negotiate with organized labor. Standards have been established by government for food and drug products, automobile safety, children's toys, clothing and hundreds of other things. "Let the buyer beware" was the operating rationale of free enterprise. Truth in packaging, disclosure of effective interest rates, consumer protection, money-back guarantees, quality control—all have been forced upon business and industry in order to protect us all from abuse.

Once an economy is planned, as ours now is, poverty cannot be explained in terms of natural laws. Once life expectancy is controlled, as ours now is, life emergence must be equally so. The continued and efficient operation of the American economy is so vital to our collective welfare that it cannot be left to chance. But the survival of American government and the rule of law is even more vital to our continued existence. Only by breaking the hold which laissez-faire exercises over family size can we exert the control necessary to an orderly and peaceful future.

In commenting upon world and national population problems, the 1968 report of Congressman Emilio Q. Dadario, Chairman of the Subcommittee on Science, Research and Development said, "Population must come under control and be stabilized at some number which civilization can agree upon. Otherwise, the best use of natural resources will be inadequate and the apocalyptic forces of disease and famine will dominate the earth." [23]

Laissez-faire no longer governs our economy and its hold on other areas of our life is fast being broken. Louis Henkin, in discussing "Changing Law for the Changing Seas," comments: "Already many challenge the basic concept of traditional law—the freedom of the seas'; we must, we are told, abandon freedom, and—as in other environments leave laissez-faire behind and move toward regulation for the common welfare." [24]

The open sea is not the only natural environment in which it has been necessary to restrict individual freedom. My family and I traveled 300 miles from Kansas City into the rural hinterland of Missouri. Our purpose was to canoe the Jack's Fork River from Alley Springs to Eminence. As we pulled into the campground which was to be our temporary home, we were greeted with these regulations:

1. DESIGNATED CAMPSITES: Camping is permitted only at designated sites equipped with a fireplace and table.
2. CAMPING: No person, party or organization shall be permitted to camp longer than 30 days during a calendar year, which includes no more than 14 days during the period June 1 to Labor Day.

3. FIRES: Fires are permitted only in the fireplace provided.
4. DIGGING: The digging, leveling of ground, or trenching around the tents at any campsites is prohibited.
5. DISTURBANCE OF PLANT OR ANIMAL LIFE: Plants or animals shall not be disturbed in any way. The driving of nails into trees or the stripping of bark, leaves or branches from trees or shrubs is prohibited.
6. UNATTENDED CAMPS: Camps may not be left unattended for more than 24 hours without specific authority of the campground Ranger. Permission must be secured in advance and will be given only when the campsite has been occupied during the 24-hour period prior to leaving the campsite unattended.
7. HOURS OF QUIET: Quiet must be maintained between the hours of 10:00 P.M. and 6:00 A.M.
8. VEHICLES: To drive, propel or park any wheeled vehicle, including trailers off the roads or parking areas is prohibited.
9. DOGS, CATS, AND PETS: All dogs, cats, and other pets must be kept on leash or under physical restrictive control at all times while in the park.
10. USE OF HYDRANTS: Cleaning fish and washing dishes or clothes at water hydrants is prohibited.
11. CLEAN CAMPS: Campers are responsible for maintaining a clean camp at all times and for cleaning their campsite, including the removal of all camping equipment, debris and refuse, before leaving.
12. DISORDERLY CONDUCT: Persons who render themselves obnoxious by disorderly conduct or bad behavior shall be subject to penalties and may be summarily removed from the Park by the Superintendent or his representative.

I can't say I was happy with all these restrictions but there was no other way to protect the river and the woods from the people, and us, from each other. Compulsion was our salvation.

A farmer may have a beautiful set of horses, possessing strength and endurance without equal. But they are useless to him in getting his land plowed until they submit to the yoke which allows them to move in the same direction at the same speed. Compulsion is the yoke by which society harnesses individual drives and ambitions to meet collective needs; unless and until the individual members of a society take the yoke upon themselves, they will never know what problems they are capable of mastering.

Eminent Domain "A man's home is his castle," Americans are often heard to say. As a recognition of the fact that within our home, we are free to do somewhat as we please, this phrase is largely correct. But it does not imply absolute freedom from restriction. Building codes for our "castles" are established and enforced by local government. The electrical wiring and the plumbing are installed by licensed workmen and inspected by public officials, both done to protect us and our neighbors from the dangers of fire and contamination. The distance from our front door to the street is decided by city engineers. The size, composition and price range of the dwelling is determined by the developer. Contracts and leases often restrict occupancy to the basic family unit made up of parents and their dependent children. Grandparents, aunts, uncles, cousins, nephews, or simply family friends are "persona non grata" on other than a temporary basis. It goes without saying that the home is not a sanctuary for illegal activities, nor does it infer immunity from punishment.

The regulations which society has imposed upon the individual dwelling place also include the right of eminent domain —the power of the government to take private property for public use without the owner's consent. Synonyms for eminent domain include such terms as expropriation, condemnation, compulsory acquisition and compulsory purchase.[25] In America, though not in all countries, compensation to the property owner is required by law. The 25th Amendment to the U.S. Constitution provides that private property shall not be "taken for public use without just compensation." The amount of compensation in any particular case is determined by the appropriate public official. If the owner does not think the amount is sufficient, he may ask for a judicial opinion on its fairness. But the owner does not have the right to refuse to sell his property.

The practice of eminent domain goes back to the seventeenth century. Evidence of its use at this time may be found in the writings of the "natural law jurists" such as Hugo Grotius and Samuel Pufendorf. At the time of Jamestown and Plymouth the English practice was to have Parliament authorize the taking of property and to prescribe the amount of payment or to provide a pseudo-judicial process, from which the property owner was excluded, to establish the amount of compensation.[26]

In the United States, the power of eminent domain belongs to the federal government as well as to that of the various states. The governmental unit which exercises eminent domain is required by law to divulge the public purpose for which the property is to be used. Once this is done the owner has no legal right to contest the legitimacy or wisdom of the decision, though he is entitled to appeal the amount of compensation.

Without the power of eminent domain, government would be severely restricted in advancing those social purposes for which it alone is responsible and on which our national welfare depends. Highway construction, slum clearance, the building of low-cost housing, promotion of industrialization, establishment of rights of way for public utilities and area beautification—these are some of the uses for which the power of eminent domain is essential.

It is apparent by now that compulsion is a daily and a desirable aspect of our collective life. To make birth control compulsory is simply a necessary extension of the process begun when man abandoned the danger of the cave for the safety of the village. Through that safety, danger has once again found us. This time, however, there is no place to run. If we are to establish justice, ensure domestic tranquility, promote the public order, and preserve our environment for our posterity, we must act quickly to reduce our numbers; not by war or disease, for both violate the values which we attach to human life. But if those values are to survive, the pregnancy epidemic must be brought under control. To do that, three things are needed. The first is our commitment to the task. Our survival is at stake, and only a total dedication of our material and mental resources can save us. If we can accomplish this fundamental reordering of our priorities, the other two survival requirements are practically assured. The second necessity for our survival kit is a contraceptive of sufficient sophistication that uncontrolled pregnancy becomes an unknown disease. The third requirement is for legislation, applied equally to all Americans, which limits the number of births. (See Chapter 10 for details.)

Writing in the April 1970 issue of *Sexology*, Richard Stiller, Associate Director of the Information Center on Population Problems asked himself the rhetorical question, "Why not, then, in the interests of all of us, restrict by law each family to two children to keep our population stable?" He then replied to his own question, "Because it won't work. Since we cannot put policemen in every bedroom, we should not put policemen in some bedrooms." [27]

The picture of the policeman in the bedroom, while designed to frighten the unthinking, is a misrepresentation of what would actually be required. More appropriately, compulsory birth control should make us think of the chemist in the laboratory or the statesman in his chambers. Surely those who advocate family planning, "wanted" children and "responsible" parenthood would not contend that parenthood is a spontaneous act committed in the bedroom rather than a decision reached jointly in less sexually designated areas of the home.

There is not a doctor in every living room nor an accountant in every study, but vaccination and taxation are compulsory. And they certainly are necessary in society's effort to maintain itself. Compulsory birth control is just as vital to our collective survival.

7 Barriers to Birth Control

What are we to make of the educated youth growing up among us that is either unconcerned about population growth, or, at the very least, unable or unwilling to apply to itself the simple arithmetic of compound interest?

—*Science*[1]

The population bomb is ticking, and the time left to defuse it may already be less than enough. At best, the margin of safety grows perilously thin. We might think, then, if all we knew of America was its population prognosis, that action was imminent and agreement was widespread. Not so. And this, by all odds, is what drives many of us to despair. Our society is caught up in what some have called a crisis of crises. All the racial, economic, political and social evils of our past have converged in our time to challenge us as never before. Because opinion is so divided as to the proper course to take on each of these problems, and because they are so interrelated, we find ourselves unable to act consistently and intelligently on any of them.

As our nation moves into the seventies, we are being challenged by the young, the black and the female segments of our population to solve the problems which confront them. And solve them we must, for they are serious and potentially explosive problems. But we must not allow the rhetoric of these groups to distort our understanding of the problems which confront all of us.

All three of these groups, to varying degrees, see the current concern with population problems as a cop-out, diverting attention from the "real" problems. To the young the "real" problem has to do with war and the military-industrial establishment which they see everywhere. Their slogans, "Hell no—we won't go" and "Make love, not war," symbolize their concern. The Women's Liberation Front insists that "women must escape from slavery and establish equality with men." Blacks argue that "racism is the Number One public enemy. To focus on any other problem insures the continuation of a racist America."

All of us who love our country (and here I refer to Adlai Stevenson's definition of patriotism as love of one's country, in contrast to nationalism which is hatred of another), must do everything in our power to remedy the problems which motivate these fellow (and lady) Americans. To be responsive to their needs, we must have the courage to speak up when we think they are wrong. Not to do so may temporarily delude them into thinking we are allies, when in fact we are only intellectual and moral cowards.

American Diversity

Americans are a diverse lot, long nurtured on the myth of the melting pot. Hardly an American is alive today who did not learn in high school history that America was a new nation, creating a new people. The 40 million immigrants who came to this country between 1850 and 1920 were said to have lost their "foreign" ways and ties. They were acculturated, assimilated and homogenized; in short Americanized. This was called "The Noble Experiment," whose rationale was best caught by Emma Lazarus' inscription for the Statue of Liberty.

Give me your tired, your poor,
Your huddled masses yearning to breathe free,
The wretched refuse of your teeming shore.
Send these, the homeless, tempest-tost to me,
I lift my lamp beside the golden door!

The experiment was a failure, and the cultural heritage of our nation is the richer for it, but its political life is more difficult, less decisive.

The majority of Americans are white, native-born and Protestant. Gendell and Zetterberg, in *A Sociological Almanac for the United States* report that 88.6% of the population is white, 83.4% native-born, and 66.2% Protestant. But this homogeneity is more apparent than real, and misleading conclusions are likely if these surface characteristics are accepted at face value.

In the first place, the nonwhite population is not composed of many different racial and ethnic groups, each with conflicting interests and objectives; hence, incapable of effective opposition to the majority. Rather, the nonwhite population is almost entirely Negro. Indians, Chinese, Japanese and other American minority groups make up approximately one-half of one percent of the nonwhite population.

This means that the large white majority is confronted by a large, black minority. When we remember that the initial and protracted relationship between these two races was that of owner and slave; when we call to mind the Civil War, precipitated by dispute over that relationship; when we witness the continuing bitterness of those to the south of the Mason-Dixon line because of their Northern-dictated post-war status; only when we have done this do we begin to realize the potential for personal and social problems inherent in the statistics of relative size.

Even this does not tell the whole story, however, for the

geographical distribution of blacks and whites is such that in some few areas, particularly the big cities and the rural South, the number of Negroes is more nearly equal that of whites. In several areas of the country Negroes even outnumber whites.

Racial Problems Currently, some black militants across the country are accusing Planned Parenthood and other family-planning organizations of genocide—the deliberate, government-sponsored extermination of all black people. Drawing parallels with Nazi Germany and its campaign to eradicate the Jew, black militants charge that birth control is a white man's plot to keep their numbers small and ultimately do away with them.

The blacks who make this charge are aware that the Negro birth rate is higher than the white, and they seem to think that, given time, this fact will transform them into a majority. Thus the birth rate becomes a political weapon. A revolutionary black publication circulated in the spring of 1970 asserted that "The black woman realizes that she must be fruitful and bear many potential warriors. This sister understands that the *YOUTH MAKE THE REVOLUTION*!" What the militants fail to realize is that at current differential growth rates, approximately 25 births and 9.4 deaths for every 1000 blacks, 16.8 births and 9.4 deaths for each 1000 whites,[2] it would take centuries for the black and white population to reach the same level. They also overlook the fact that should the white population interpret the higher birth rate of the Negro as a threat, it could step up its own fertility, thereby making the Negro population an even smaller part of the total.

I dare say no black leader, whether militant or moderate, believes that we can wait to solve our racial problems until the two groups are equal in size. We certainly do not have that kind of time to bring our population growth under control.

Blacks also fear that birth control, once widely accepted, will be used differently on blacks than on whites. This fear grows out of the fact that American institutions—"The Establishment" as they are presently known—have usually discriminated on the basis of race, with unpleasant consequences for Negroes.

If I were young and black today, I most certainly would be militant and I too would cry genocide. I would seize whatever issues were available to make myself heard. I would inject the racial question into every discussion of national priorities and programs, hoping desperately to elicit an adequate response to the problems of the American Negro, determined that, should I fail, others would suffer with me.

The *Report of the National Advisory Commission on Civil Disorders* should have convinced white America that it can no longer ignore or pacify black America. By the same token, black militants should realize that no government legitimizes the protest of a group which it plans to exterminate. Had the *Report* categorically condemned the riots, giving no attention to the historical, sociological and psychological conditions out of which they grew; had it played up black extremism while overlooking white racism; had it not found white America guilty of individual discrimination and institutional exclusion; had it, in short, read more like an attack than a confession, then blacks could justify their charge of genocide.

It is a two-fold tragedy that black militants oppose birth control programs. First because their opposition most hurts those they want to help. Add together the number of black women frightened or intimidated into refusing birth control help, the unwanted children born as a result, the accompanying economic and family tensions, then the magnitude of error in the militant position is evident.

One of the major arguments against the charge of genocide is the question of quality vs. quantity. This is the basis of Dr. Frederick C. Green's fight against the charges. Dr. Green is a black man and director of Pediatric Ambulatory Care at Roosevelt Hospital in New York. "What good is it to have 10 or 15 children under undesirable conditions in which they are not able to develop their total potential?" he asks.[3]

Most militants brush off the hard facts concerning the effects on a woman of a large number of births. They also overlook the risks of bearing an abnormal child. Premature births are extremely high among very young mothers and those who bear children at capacity levels. Consider these statistics:

1. Premature infants have two to three times as many physical defects and 50% more illnesses than full term babies.
2. Mental retardation is 16 times higher among premature babies.
3. A premature infant is six times more likely to die during the first four weeks of life than a child born of a full term pregnancy.[4]
4. The infant mortality rate for blacks is twice that of whites in the United States.[5]

Nationally syndicated columnist Carl T. Rowan, himself a Negro, asks: "What kind of black pride is it, what kind of militancy is it, that asks black women to accept physical abuse and sometimes degradation to produce large numbers of children when the odds are that many of them will be retarded and bear other afflictions?"

In testifying on behalf of a family planning bill before the Health Subcommittee of the Senate Committee on Labor and Public Welfare in December 1969, Negro Congresswoman Shirley Chisholm (D-N.Y.) said:

> I know that in my own Bedford-Stuyvesant community, black women are glad to get direction in the area of family planning. I know that thousands of black women have been maimed by botched abortions because they couldn't get the family planning help that white women could get. I have heard some repercussions that family planning is a form of genocide. But the people this would affect—in Harlem and Bedford-Stuyvesant—think otherwise. I

have had hundreds of black women come to me over the past ten years because they wanted family planning.[6]

Several years ago in Pittsburgh a group of 70 women forced local militant William "Bouie" Haden to back off the genocide issue. Later, in the same city, Monsignor Charles Owen Rice joined the anti-birth control crusade. "Strange," he said, "there are few birth control clinics in white areas." Planned Parenthood officials answered this by saying that the areas were predominately Catholic, a fact that the Monsignor should have known.[7]

Secondly, the militant charge of genocide is a tragedy because, while it hurts those they want to hurt, it does so in a way which none of us, black or white, can survive. No matter what one's color or attitude, we can survive without air for only a few minutes, without water for only a few days, without food for only a few weeks, without purpose for only a few, unhappy years.

One thing which lends credence to the genocide charge made by militant blacks is the fact that the United States has never ratified the United Nations' Convention on Genocide which was adopted by most nations after World War II. This document was drafted primarily to ensure that nothing like Hitler's campaign against the Jews would ever again be undertaken. While sympathetic with the intentions of this document, the U.S. government contends that signing it would abdicate authority over internal affairs to foreign governments. Whatever the reasons, however, the present state of black-white relations in this country demands that the United States ratify the Genocide Convention. Blacks can never trust the government until it does, and they will continue their opposition to programs essential to our mutual welfare.

Some blacks actually believe that the federal government has a contingency plan already worked out to eliminate the minority threat to internal security. John A. Williams' 1967 novel, *The Man Who Cried I Am,* described the "King Alfred Plan" which was supposed to be a government outline of what would be done in the event of a race war. According to this fictitious plan, the country was divided into 10 geographical areas, and in the event of widespread racial conflict, an eight-hour countdown would begin to end with the extermination of black people. Our government must do all in its power to demonstrate the utter impossibility of any such action ever occurring. Until it does, charges of genocide will continue to reduce the effectiveness of all programs designed to benefit all Americans.

Black militants who charge birth control advocates with genocide would do well to consider the Jew. During World War II, 6 million European Jews were slaughtered by an insane Nazi regime bent on the annihilation of all Jews. If any people have cause to be concerned about genocide, it is the Jew. Yet of all ethnic and religious groups in America, Jews voluntarily have the lowest birth rate. Studies have shown that Jewish families want and have smaller families than Protestants or Catholics.[8] At the same time, American Jews have a higher standard of living than any other minority group. By keeping their completed family size at approximately two children, Jewish families have been able to concentrate their resources on educational and employment opportunities. The Jews have also been able to achieve a high degree of social, economic and political power.

Geographic Differences The large percentage of "native-born" Americans mentioned earlier also contains latent heterogeneity which acts as a barrier to the acceptance of birth control. Lumped together in one amorphous mass we find Tennessee Hillbillies, Oakies and Arkies, Mexican-Americans of the Southwest, the old aristocracy of the Southeast, Little Sicily, Chinatown, Spanish and Negro Harlem, religious-communal societies, Greenwich Village, the French Quarter, Division Street, Madison Avenue, Hungry Horse, Montana, and Houston, Texas. We find the "jet set" and the unemployed, the illiterate and the erudite, the rich and the poor, the Country Club Plaza and the Public Housing Project. The fisherman of Maine has little in common with the rancher of Montana. The Black Hills of South Dakota condition people differently than the Smokey Mountains of North Carolina.

There is an infinity of difference in the knowledge of the world, its problems and prospects, found among these diverse people. Some have no understanding of population pressures because they live in areas of few people. Many of them think of their state, county or city as underpopulated and lay plans to increase its size. While it is true that some parts of our country could support more people at an acceptable level, it is important that our nation maintain vast areas of low density where the land is allowed to remain in its original or present state. Not only is it necessary in order to preserve wildlife, both animal and vegetable, but it allows the earth to heal itself, to act on the industrial and individual poisons urban man foists upon it. Our land and our nation simply cannot survive the extension of its cities and its crises. Yet the U.S. Soil Conservation Service reported that the amount of privately owned rural land dropped by nearly 15 million acres between 1958 and 1967. Thus an area almost as large as West Virginia was victimized by urban sprawl.[9]

Attitudes toward birth control vary widely in the different sections of America. There are Kansas wheat farmers and Mississippi cotton growers who plant hybrid strains plentifully nourished with man-made fertilizers, yet think of human birth control as "unnatural." Washington officials and Utah ranchers limit agricultural production in order to preserve price stability, yet both define family planning in terms of everyone doing as they please. "Planning in this case," said the hare to Alice, "means exactly what I want it to mean; nothing more, nothing less."

Doublethink has become the order of the day. We can, in one breath, talk about a planned economy, city planning, traffic control, price ceilings, zoning regulations, land use, and know that all these necessitate restrictions on individual initiative and direction. Yet when we, in the next breath, mention family planning, birth control, zero population growth, population control, we assume just the opposite—that every individual can do just as he pleases. And then we move beyond doublethink to the comically absurd position that both types of "planning" will achieve the same end. We are trying desperately to have our cake and eat it too, but experience and the laws of physics demonstrate its impossibility.

Economic Obstacles In the early 1960s America rediscovered its poor. For the first time since the thirties, poverty became a social and political issue. Most Americans assumed that the wave of prosperity which swept the nation after World War II had carried everyone in its wake. But Michael Harrington shocked Americans with his description of *The Other America,* a nation of poverty in the midst of plenty.[10] Following his book, an attack was mounted by Washington to eradicate poverty in this country. Known as the War on Poverty, its strategy was designed to include the 20 to 50 million poor in programs of job training, purchasing skills and attitude change. The battle plan failed because it was ill conceived and poorly executed. And the poor find themselves still largely without services or opportunity. One service they are still without is birth control.

It is estimated that five million American women today are denied birth control services because they are poor. Until recently, welfare regulations prohibited the offering of contraceptive advice or devices to the poor. The poor were victims of flagrant economic discrimination; because they could not pay, they were forced to bear unwanted children. For years the response of welfare workers and charity doctors to the pleas of poor women who had just delivered a child was, "See you next year." Thus mother and child went "home" to a filthy, overcrowded tenement infested with vermin or an isolated rural shanty devoid of sanitary facilities. Condemned to compulsory pregnancy or to death at the hands of an incompetent abortionist, these women paid dearly for their poverty. The middle-class woman, however, who could afford a private physician was advised of contraceptive precautions and if she found herself undesirably pregnant, that too could be taken care of.

Many, though by no means all, of the repressive welfare laws governing birth control have been repealed. But the attitudes and habits of the poor and those who supposedly help them will be a long time catching up.

Some Americans blame socialism for our population problems. As one writer put it, "socialism always creates ultimately an imbalance between the number of people living and their food supply which results in hunger or famine. There is in this sense therefore always a problem of overpopulation under socialism. Hunger is chronic and endemic to socialism." [11]

What a curious commentary on intelligence that socialist countries blame their population problems on capitalism, while capitalist countries blame theirs on socialism. It's a little like two small boys, each accusing the other of breaking the cookie jar, though they both had their hands in it.

Religious Barriers There are also religious barriers to birth control. The fact that two thirds of the American population is Protestant might lead the casual observer to think that opinion on birth control would be fairly uniform across the country. Not so. "Protestant" is a rather loosely defined term which originally served to designate those denominations tracing their origin to the religious schism of the Reformation. As used in the United States, this term has served as a catch-all category including any and all non-Jewish, non-Catholic elaborations on the Judeo-Christian tradition. According to Frank Mead's *Handbook of Denominations in the United States,* there are presently in this country more than 240 such denominations, with names ranging from the little known Duck River and Kindred Associations of Baptists and Fire Baptized Holiness Church of God of the Americas to the more prosaic Methodist Church and Lutheran Church (Missouri Synod) and with doctrines ranging from the "liberal" position of the

Unitarians to the ultra-fundamentalism of the various Pentecostal bodies. The size of the various denominations also varies greatly, ranging from the nearly 9 million members and 40,472 churches comprising the Methodist Church to the 210 members and nine churches of the Church of God in Christ.[12]

The positions taken on birth control by Protestant churches are almost as varied as their names and numbers.

Earl Reeves, in an article called "The Population Explosion and Christian Concern" says, "It is impossible to describe any one position on birth control as representing the official Protestant view." [13] Most of the major Protestant groups, however, officially endorse birth control. The Board of Christian Social Concerns of the United Methodist Church adopted a Statement of Responsible Parenthood in October 1969. It read in part:

> The United Methodist Church calls its members and challenges society to responsible parenthood. This necessitates the constructive use of sexuality, creativity, and technologies which make possible the achievement of conception control and regulation of population levels.

Acceptance of the birth control philosophy and techniques by Protestant groups is a fairly new development. Arthur Matthews, writing in *Christianity Today,* said "Rome merely believes what the Protestants did until several decades ago." [14] Even though the official bodies of many Protestant churches have recently issued enlightened statements on birth control most local congregations remain either ignorant of the new viewpoint or opposed to it. In an excellent review of *Birth Control in the Modern World,* Elizabeth Draper indicts Protestant Churches for "making the exploration of matters concerned with reproduction as well as fertility control unpopular and unsupported." [15]

The Protestant Church in America is divided on the subject of contraception and birth control. On the one hand are progressive statements and on the other, traditional attitudes and actions.

Though America is two thirds Protestant, the Catholic Church has had much more impact on the birth control movement. On November 13, 1921, the first birth control conference in America was to be held at the Town Hall in New York City. Margaret Sanger, originator of the birth control movement, was to speak. But before the meeting could begin, it was broken up by the police acting on orders from a man who said, according to Margaret Sanger's autobiography *My Fight for Birth Control,* that he was secretary to the Archbishop of the Roman Catholic Diocese of New York.[16]

This was only the first round in a long and continuing fight between what we could now call the Pope and the Pill. The Catholic Church teaches that marital sex is for procreation only. Coitus for any other purpose, particularly if action is taken to prevent conception, is a sin. Hopes ran high in the mid-sixties that the Papal Study Commission on Birth Control, convened first by Pope John and then by Pope Paul, would modify the Catholic rejection of contraception. But it did not happen. On July 25, 1968, Pope Paul issued *Humanae Vitae,* his encyclical on birth control. Despite the fact that the majority of members of the two study commissions had endorsed a liberalization of the Catholic position, the Pope reaffirmed the Church's opposition:

> Nonetheless the Church, calling men back to the observance of the natural law, as interpreted by their *constant* [emphasis added] doctrine, teaches that each and every marriage act (*quilbet matrimonii usus*) must remain open to the transmission of life.

The Encyclical itself demonstrates that the Pope was more concerned with upholding the authority of the Church than with solving the problems of personal and social overpopulation. The Encyclical asks:

> Would not a revision of the ethical norms, in force up to now, seem to be advisable, especially when it is considered that they cannot be observed without sacrifices, sometimes heroic sacrifices?

But it then declares:

> . . . . of such laws the Church was not the author, nor consequently can she be their arbiter; she is only their depository and their interpreter, without ever being able to declare to be licit that which is not so by reason of its intimate and unchangeable opposition to the true good of man.

When other institutions refuse to change with the times, we call them irrelevant; if they cop-out by pleading that they don't make the rules, but only interpret them, we call them an irresponsible and unresponsive bureaucracy.

In justifying his opposition to birth control, the Pope speculates that a man who employs contraceptives may lose respect for the woman and use her for his selfish enjoyment. But the man could as easily tire of so many children or a wife-mother so busy she had no time for him. Both are speculation, but they lead to different contraceptive policies. The Encyclical also gives evidence that the Catholic Church believes morality can be sustained only if people are afraid to do otherwise. In considering contraception, the Pope says, ". . . how wide and easy a road would thus be opened up toward conjugal infidelity and the general lowering of morality." The Pope apparently feels that only fear of pregnancy is sufficient to maintain sexual morality.

The Encyclical does reaffirm Catholic approval of the rhythm method of birth control:

> The Church teaches that it is then licit to take into account the natural rhythms immanent in the generative functions, for the use of marriage in the in-

> fecund periods only, and in this way to regulate birth without offending the moral principles which have been mentioned earlier.

But Vatican roulette, as critics have dubbed it, discriminates against the uneducated and makes no allowance for the spontaneity and impulsiveness of human sexuality.

Those who advocate the rhythm method, however, turn the argument around and blame the husband and wife if they find it unsatisfactory. The Catholic-sponsored 2nd International Symposium on Rhythm made these observations: "To the couple whose marriage is unhappy the method may present major problems, but to those whose marriage is happy the problems will be no more than minor." A medical doctor said "Whenever I have studied a Catholic couple who found the rhythm method intolerable and who feared it would disrupt their marriage, without exception I found them mismated, with personality problems that would have threatened the marriage had they belonged to another faith." [17]

The article concluded that "rather than a population explosion in this country, we are witnessing a copulation explosion." [18]

Many Catholics have been driven by economic and family considerations to violate the Church's teaching on birth control. Recent studies indicate that a majority of Catholics use contraceptives at some time in their married life. However, this use most often occurs after the birth of several children, and while helping to alleviate family problems involving unwanted and unneeded children, such late use does little to solve the nation's problem of too many people.

The Jewish position on birth control resembles both the Protestant and the Catholic. The Rabbinical Association of America in 1958 stated that Orthodox Jews condemned birth control methods used by the husband. Birth control measures were permissible, however, if the health of the woman were in danger, but only through direct consultation of medical and rabbinical authorities.[19]

The Reform and the Conservative Jewish sects on the other hand define the procreative "duty" of Jews as two children. Since the mid-thirties, both groups have urged "proper education in contraception and birth control as a means of enhancing rather than destroying the spiritual values inherent in the family and of achieving the advancement and welfare of mankind." [20]

According to a study entitled *Fertility and Family Planning in the United States,* a large majority of American women in 1960, of all religious backgrounds, were found to favor birth control; 96% of Protestants, 85% of Catholics and 98% of Jews. However, when the group favoring birth control was divided into those "strongly" and "moderately" in favor, only 57% of Protestants, 25% of Catholics and 83% of Jews were "strongly" in favor. Of the Catholic wives who were favorable toward birth control, 33% were specifically for rhythm rather than some other method. Only 5% of Protestants and no Jews favored rhythm.[21]

It was found that American wives, both Protestant and Catholic, expected to have more children in 1960 than in 1955. This increase was primarily among the lesser educated women, but the expectations of the better educated wives did not decline during this five-year period.[22] Five percent of the wives wanted only one child. About 12% wanted five or more.[23] When the women were asked, "If you could live your life over again, and have everything just the way you would like it to be, how many children would you have in all?" more said they wanted four children than any other single number. The average number wanted was 3.7.[24]

An Irish Catholic couple had been married about 11 years and lived in a large eastern city. The wife was thirty-four and had already given birth to seven children. "I want to have at least ten," she said, "but I'll be happy to accept as large a family as fate gives me. I wouldn't want to have a smaller family, because I love children, and I think children in small families miss much of the give and take of learning to live together."

A devout Protestant wife of thirty-two and mother of five wanted and expected to have twelve children. As she explained, "I just enjoy them. I feel you are blessed by the Lord when you have more children." [25]

Of all the women interviewed, 81% had used some form of birth control. But usage was found to increase with the number of pregnancies. By religion, the Jews were most likely to use contraceptives before the first pregnancy and Catholics were the least likely. Though better than eight in ten wives had used some form of birth control, most had begun its use only after several births. Apparently, then, they were motivated more by desperation than by anticipation. Contraception became their last chance for avoiding ridiculously large families without sacrificing their marital relationship.

Birth control in America has been and continues to be severely restricted by religious opposition. A case in point are the letters to the editor of the Southern Baptist *Home Missions* magazine which ran an article of mine in 1968 asking, "Should the Government Limit Births?" A letter from Ohio said: "The article by Ed Chasteen was the most pagan I have ever read in a SBC publication. Mr. Chasteen's reasoning is about as Christian as was that of Hitler and his followers." Another letter, written from Arkansas, stated that "the kindest thing I can say is that the ultrasocialistic and atheistic objectives are frank and undisguised. To be quite frank, some plain old unprintable Anglo-Saxon words might best describe my feelings toward Chasteen's article and your editorial policy permitting it."

Another letter ended with this characteristically open-minded invitation to social responsibility: "Responsible Southern Baptists must immediately and unmistakably repudiate this professor and your own editorial folly. As a Christian and Southern Baptist deacon I hold that no one who condones or defends those presentations as Christian thinking has any right to a church-supported job as preacher, professor or editor."

Some religious people quote the Bible to justify their opposition to birth control. Their favorite verse is, "Be fruitful and multiply and replenish the earth." The best Biblical response to this is the statement from Ecclesiastes: "To everything there is a season, and a time to every purpose under heaven." The "everything" for which there is a time obviously includes birth control. It is also instructive to point out that had we done as well at keeping other Biblical commandments as we have at multiplying, the kingdom would have long ago come on earth as it is in heaven.

The opposition of the single-verse Christian (or Jew, etc.) to anything is a travesty on religion. Those who pick out whatever verse seems to support their position rather than trying to relate the entire scripture to the problem are using religion as other men use money and power—to get their own way.

Because of the many ethical and religious issues involved in a population control policy, the Church will, to a large extent, determine whether we act in time. I regret to say that a review of Church history does not give much reason for optimism. From the feudal period, when the Church sanctioned serfdom and special privilege, until the present, we find the Church usually opposed to social change.

The Church is now offered the opportunity to redeem both itself and humanity through its active support of philosophies and programs designed to check the cancerous growth of uncontrolled population. The Church dare not remain silent or uninformed. To do nothing offers temporary safety; to oppose brings transient popularity; to champion a good cause is to be relevant and humanly redemptive.

Psychological and Social Barriers

In additional to racial, economic and religious barriers to birth control, there are many psychological and social barriers. The desire for at least one child of each sex undoubtedly causes some parents to have more children than they would have liked. A family we have known for a good many years in another state now has five girls, though when John and Marge were first married they wanted one child of each sex. Since their first daughter was born, they have been trying for a boy. This problem may one day be overcome by medical techniques which make it possible to determine the sex of a child before birth. Adoption of a child offers a present remedy for this problem, while at the same time reducing rather than increasing the number of unwanted children.

Some women have children because they are lonely or they feel rejected by their husbands. Some parents have many children because they see them as their hedge against an insecure old age. Others want a large family because they fear a small one might be wiped out by natural or man-made disaster. Some parents fear that an only child will be warped emotionally. One 27-year-old wife, married only a few months and with no children, said she wanted six or eight and was sure she would have that many. "I wouldn't want to have fewer, because I think children are better behaved, learn more and are happier in large families."

Another psychological barrier to birth control concerns the attitude of some husbands toward female contraceptives. A husband may refuse to let his wife use contraceptives because she then enjoys the same sexual freedom as he does. For the husband who is insecure and/or unfaithful, this may be an unwelcome development. If he feels that only the fear of pregnancy will keep her from playing around, he is not likely to endorse her use of birth control.

The tax deductions allowed for children, though certainly not a direct inducement to parenthood, undoubtedly lead some prospective parents to vote "yes" rather than "no," as might be the case if there were a tax penalty instead.

Opposition to birth control also is built into the American economy. The baby food and clothing industry, toy makers, school equipment manufacturers, home builders, all have a vested interest in high fertility. With our present level of affluence, so do auto makers, cosmetic salesmen, fashion designers, record distributors and textbook companies, for infants soon become adolescents, and their appetites are insatiable. Business has long assumed that it had a "right" to expand through continuous increases in customers and workers. Accordingly, business has long supported a high birth rate. The American business sector has a mania for development which necessitates a constantly expanding population. To the businessman all of nature is a resource awaiting his development. The more people there are, the easier for the businessman to convince others that another part of the environment should be designated as a resource for exploitation and profit.

The Comstock Laws Whether Americans practice birth control is as much a result of law and social policy as of parental desire. If those laws and policies reward large families, then families will be large. On the other hand, if those policies penalize large families, then families will be small. American government, from the courthouse to the White House, has always encouraged large families. First as colonists and settlers, then as laborers, now as consumers and polluters, a pronatalist governmental policy has ruled the land.

These policies were embodied most obviously in the 1873 Comstock Laws which branded contraceptives as indecent and prohibited their display or sale; employed currently by the states of Massachusetts, Wisconsin and others to intimidate and prosecute birth control advocates, these repressive laws are as much responsible for America's population problem as the reproductive habits of its people. Perhaps more so, since the laws give birth to the habit.

Anthony Comstock, a grocery clerk and one of ten children, was made director of the Society for the Suppression of Vice around 1870. For more than 40 years he acted as the self-appointed censor of American morals condemning literary classics, commercial pornography and birth control as indecent and obscene.

Comstock's activities and influence were described as follows:

> This was the man who went to the halls of Congress in 1873 and lobbied through both houses, with less

> than a total of one hour of debate, the law that—with few and relatively trifling changes—still governs "obscenity" in the mails. It was hurried through in the closing hours of a hectic session, the final vote coming about 2:00 A.M. on a Sunday morning, although the clock was stopped to preserve the fiction that it was still Saturday.[26]

This law was directed almost exclusively against contraceptives, and it established the official attitude and position from which we have not yet escaped. The law read:

TIT. 18. CRIMES AND CRIMINAL PROCEDURE
Ch. 71. Obscenity

Section 1461. Mailing obscene or crime-inciting matter.

> Every obscene, lewd, lascivious, or filthy book, pamphlet, picture, paper, letter, writing, print, or other publication of an indecent character; and
>
> Every article or thing designed, adapted or intended for preventing conception or producing abortion, or for any indecent or immoral use; and
>
> Every article, instrument, substance, drug, medicine, or thing which is advertised or described in a manner calculated to lead another to use or apply it for preventing conception or producing abortion, or for any indecent or immoral purpose; and
>
> Every written or printed card, letter, circular, book, pamphlet, advertisement, or notice of any kind giving information, directly or indirectly, where, or how, or from whom, or by what means any of such mentioned matters, articles, or things may be obtained or made, or where or by whom any act or operation of any kind for the procuring or producing of abortion will be done or performed, or how or by what means conception may be pre-

> vented or abortion produced, whether sealed or unsealed; and
>
> Every paper, writing, advertisement, or representation that any article, instrument, substance, drug, medicine, or thing may, or can, be used or applied for preventing conception or producing abortion, or for any indecent or immoral purpose; and
>
> Every description calculated to induce or incite a person to so use or apply any such article, instrument, substance, drug, medicine, or thing—
>
> Is declared to be nonmailable matter and shall not be conveyed in the mails or delivered from any post office or by any letter carrier.
>
> Whoever knowingly uses the mail for the mailing, carriage in the mails, or delivery of anything declared by this section to be nonmailable, or knowingly causes to be delivered by mail according to the direction thereon, or at the place at which it is directed to be delivered by the person to whom it is addressed, or knowingly takes any such thing from the mails for the purpose of circulating or disposing thereof, shall be fined not more than $5,000 or imprisoned not more than five years, or both, for the first such offense, and shall be fined not more than $10,000 or imprisoned not more than ten years or both, for each such offense thereafter.[27]

What a tragedy that Comstock lumped pornography and contraception together. He apparently believed there was something inherently evil about the human body, particularly those areas associated with reproduction and sexual stimulation. Certainly since his day this attitude has pervaded American thought and action. Out of this national paranoia has come our system of medical and social rewards. The person who finds a cure for disease is lauded. Hospitals are dedicated in his name and his opinion is sought on issues for which he has not the slightest qualification. The person who advocates or perfects birth control which the cure made necessary, is dismissed as a dirty old man (or woman). Contrast the public attitude toward Margaret Sanger and Jonas Salk.

Because those concerned with birth control are more punished than rewarded, the level of contraceptive technology in America is unbelievably crude when compared to that in other medical areas. This constitutes one of the major barriers to extensive and effective birth control. (See Chapter 8 for further discussion on this point.)

When all is said and done, the biggest barrier to birth control is probably the ignorance of the educated. It is simply unbelievable. My own college experience is a perfect example. I graduated from an east Texas college in 1957, having taken courses in biology, marriage and family, and physical education. Yet when I graduated I could not even spell contraception, let alone apply it. Heaven only knows how many are in the same boat today. One recent study done at a major university found that 84 percent of those interviewed thought that it was desirable to limit family size, but most of them wanted three or more children. Almost half of those interviewed, including biology students, thought that sterilization interfered with sexual abilities. Only six percent of the men favored vasectomy once the desired family size had been attained, and only two percent of the women chose tubal ligation. These operations were poorly understood and not at all appealing as means of limiting family size.

The authors of this study are concerned about "the probability that proponents of voluntary sterilization are backing a hopeless or nearly hopeless cause." They conclude with two questions, the first of which introduced this chapter. "But what are we to make of the educated youth growing up among us that is either unconcerned about population growth or, at the very least, unable or unwilling to apply to itself the simple arithmetic of compound interest? And what, if any, are the prospects for improved sex education when ignorance about the reproductive system is widespread even among those who should know best?" [28]

8 Stone-Age Contraception

Many demographers believe that if significant reductions in population growth are to be achieved there must be a technological breakthrough in contraception similar to that in food production.

—*The New York Times,* an editorial [1]

In a society which yearly consumes billions of tablets and oceans of medicinal liquids, all having different brand and scientific names, mention of "The" Pill is instantly recognized and understood. It's as if Americans everywhere had accepted a little three-letter nondescript, almost useless word to sum up the far-reaching consequences of the oral contraceptive.

From its current widespread discussion and use, contraception seems to have been both invented and perfected in the Pill. In the political and social sense, that is certainly true. President Eisenhower disclaimed any governmental responsibility for birth control and family planning in the late 1950s. But the three Presidents of the sixties—Kennedy, Johnson and Nixon—endorsed family planning programs and encouraged government to move in this direction. Medically and individually, however, birth control is as old as Man himself. Had our ancestors not practiced some form of contraception and birth control, we would today be packed together like multiplying rabbits in an ever-shrinking cage. Over the entire surface of the earth, human beings would be stacked hundreds of miles deep, and the combined weight of this insanely proliferated humanity would wretch our planet from its orbit, flinging it to an eternal death in the far reaches of outer space.

Abortion, infanticide, abstention, continence, coitus interruptus, insertion of a foreign object into the uterus, sterilization, condoms, medicinal concoctions—all have been used for thousands of years in order to avoid pregnancy. The Abelians, in the early days of Christianity, had sexual intercourse only during the woman's menstrual cycle. The Masai men believed that their wives were fertile when a certain tree was in bloom and avoided them at that time. The Nandi tribe of East Africa and the Isleta Indians of New Mexico recognized infertile periods and regulated intercourse accordingly. Physicians in second-century Rome calculated and recommended the safe period. Rumanians used to avoid intercourse during menstruation because they thought it to be a fertile period.[2]

Sterilization of the male, usually by castration, has been used for centuries along with sterilization of the female, usually following childbirth. Plugging of the upper vagina with sponges or other mechanical barriers was known as a contraceptive agent as early as 1500 B.C. Mesopotamians used cup-shaped barriers made from pomegranates and fitted over the cervix in the sixth century A.D. Primitive people also used various douching solutions to prevent conception.

A formula for contraceptive preparation was discovered in Egyptian writings which date back 1000 years. Egyptians also had medical prescriptions for such substances as honey, gum and oil which, placed in the vagina, interfered with conception. One specific contraceptive, made of pulverized crocodile dung in fermented mucilage, honey and sodium carbonate, was sprinkled in the vulva. One dose was supposed to prevent pregnancy from one to three years.[3] At later times and in other parts of the world, elephant dung was used. Elizabeth Draper's excellent review of *Birth Control in the Modern World* says the dung plugged the entrance to the uterus and the acid in it killed the sperm released by the male. Other early contraceptives mentioned by Draper include onion and peppermint juice; leek-seeds; blackpills containing tannic acid used in Sumatra; rock salt dipped in oil, and mustard seed tampons used by Hindu women; chopped cabbage leaves, oil and tar used in Jordan; peppermint combined with honey and gum cedar and other ingredients in ancient Rome.[4]

The principle of intrauterine contraception, on which present IUDs are based, is of ancient origin. For centuries, Arabian and Turkish camel drivers inserted stones into the uterus of their camels in order to prevent pregnancy during long and dangerous trips across the desert. The Dahomey tribe of West Africa used the crushed tubercled root to plug the vagina. The Easter Islands inhabitants used seaweed while Central African tribes used rags and grass. A ball of opium placed in the vagina was used in Sumatra. The ancient Jews and the women of Constantinople used a sponge dipped in lemon juice as an intrauterine device. Disks made of oiled bamboo tissue paper were used in Japan and melted beeswax, by German-Hungarian women.[5]

In modern times, the principle of the intrauterine device was first applied to human populations around 1920. At that time, Dr. Graefenberg of Germany developed a ring made of silk and silver for use as an intrauterine device.

The search for an oral contraceptive began long ago. Chinese women in 2700 B.C. swallowed quicksilver. Women in the Middle Ages ingested liquid lead. Both served to prevent pregnancy either by killing the woman or causing serious internal damage. Recipes for oral contraceptives are numerous in the records of early civilizations from all over the world. Drinking extracts, usually very hot, from various kinds of trees and roots, egg yokes, foam from a camel's mouth, water used by smiths to cool their metals, gunpowder dissolved in liquid, moderate doses of arsenic, all have been used by women seeking to remedy what was to them a painful and sometimes fatal condition.[6]

These early oral contraceptives sought primarily to flush the body, either ridding it of the fertilized egg after conception or disturbing the sexual physiology in such a way as to inhibit the union of sperm and egg. The first suggestions that pregnancy could be averted by controlling ovulation came in 1856 in a book by J. Soule, an American physician.[7]

This brief review of contraceptive history illustrates the fact that all of the principles and most of the techniques of modern contraception were known hundreds and thousands of years ago. Prior to 1960 only conventional and historical methods were being used: diaphragms, condoms, vaginal creams, jellies and tablets, rhythm, spermicides. The failure rate from these methods due to inept and inconsistent use as well as their lack of medical sophistication has always been high.

In 1960 the oral contraceptive pill was made available and in 1962 the IUD was introduced. Though the principles of both are ancient the application was advanced, or so it seemed at the time. In early 1970 approximately 8 million American women were taking the Pill and one million used the IUD. Of the world's 770 million fertile women, about 13 million use the oral contraceptive and 7 million use the intrauterine device. With such a poor usage record, is it any wonder that we have a world epidemic of pregnancy?

Birth Control Methods

Contraceptive methods may be divided into three types: biological, mechanical and chemical. Before discussing them, however, we should distinguish between contraception and birth control. Though often used interchangeably in conversation, they are not synonymous. Contraception literally means opposed to, against, to interfere with conception, the union of egg and sperm. Contraception then does not allow the sexual union of male and female to result in pregnancy. Birth control, on the other hand, is a much more inclusive term. Anything which prevents or terminates pregnancy would be a method of birth control, as would the killing of the infant after birth and the castration or sterilization of adults. Marriage customs, sexual taboos and religious rites might also fall under the general heading of birth control.

Sterilization Birth control methods obviously include contraception but are not confined to it. In America, two of the most used birth control methods, exclusive of contraception, are sterilization of both male and female and abortion. The male sterilization procedure is known as vasectomy. It is a 15-minute operation performed under a local anesthetic, easily done in the privacy of a doctor's office. The procedure is to make a small incision on either side of the scrotum and to sever the vas deferens which conducts the sperm from the penis into the female vagina during ejaculation. Cutting this duct does not in any way interfere with sexual desire or performance on the part of the male. It is a 100 percent effective method of birth control, provided the doctor, after cutting the vas deferens, folds one end back and ties it securely to prevent the ends from growing back together. For several days following the operation sexual intercourse should be avoided. Approximately one week from the date of the surgery, a sperm count should be taken to determine whether the seminal fluid contains sperm. It will not if the operation was successful, and the male will then be sterile.

A man in San Rafael, California describes his vasectomy:

> In my case my wife and I decided we had had enough children and were tired of all the restraints to avoid more. Besides we enjoyed our sex life and disliked these restraints.
>
> It was a simple operation and relatively painless, only taking a few minutes. That was twenty years ago and we have had all these years since of thoroughly enjoyable and certainly undiminished sex life and vigor. My wife has thanked me in countless ways for taking her fears and worries away and making our sex life such a joyful thing. No pills, no calendars, just enjoyment—and still going strong at fifty-eight.

Vasectomy is legal in all 50 states, although Connecticut and Utah limit it to medical necessity.[8] Many doctors, but by no means all, require a conference with both husband and wife before agreeing to perform the operation. Since the operation is considered to be permanent, many medical doctors are reluctant to suggest it and are cautious in performing it, lest they find themselves later with an irate ex-patient and a possible law suit. Doctors, however, have reported 50 to 80 percent success in reversing the operation.[9] Nevertheless, the present level of technology dictates that vasectomy must be considered permanent. Several experimental techniques are now under study which would make it reversible. One of the most technically promising involves the insertion of a valve in the vas deferens. Working on the same principle as a shut-off valve on a pipeline, this technique would make it possible to open and close the sperm duct at will. The valve would be inserted just beneath the surface of the scrotum and could be switched on and off by use of a magnet on the surface of the skin. Whether the valve was on or off at any given time could also be determined by use of the magnet.

Though this development is technically promising, it is unlikely ever to get extensive use. Unlike the severing of the vas deferens, which requires only one visit to a doctor, this procedure would require several. It would also require that the man be viligant enough to know the position of the valve at all times. He would also have to keep the magnet readily available, if he were to do the opening and closing himself, or schedule an appointment with his doctor if the doctor had to change the position of the valve. Either way, usage would be affected and effectiveness would be diminished.

Approximately 100,000 vasectomies are performed in the United States each year. An estimated 1,500,000 living American men have had themselves voluntarily sterilized.[10] The Association for Voluntary Sterilization with headquarters in New York City has a referral panel of more than 1600 cooperating physicians across the country to whom it refers men interested in vasectomy. The number of men choosing this method of birth control is growing as the unreliability and undesirability of contraceptives becomes more apparent. It is unlikely, however, that more than a handful of the sexually active and fertile American men will ever elect to have a vasectomy.

Surgical birth control on the female consists of tying the Fallopian tubes (tubal ligation), severing the tubes, removal of the womb or ovaries and abortion. Tying of the tubes is now rarely done because it is difficult to reinflate them so as to allow conception again, yet the possibility of spontaneous repair is always present. Compared to tubal ligation, the surgical cutting of the Fallopian tubes is more reliable, similar to vasectomy in the male, and currently the method used most. In the female, Fallopian tubes carry the egg from the ovary to its position in the uterus where it is available for fertilization by the sperm. When the tubes are cut, it is no longer possible for the egg to get to the uterus, hence pregnancy is impossible. Severing of the tubes is a relatively minor operation if performed, as it usually is, immediately following childbirth. However, a nonpregnant woman can be sterilized at any time either by incision through the abdomen or, if necessary, through the vagina.

Since female sexual anatomy and physiology are more involved than the male, greater medical risks are run by operating on the woman. In the great majority of cases, vasectomy is safer and less complicated than either tubal ligation or severing of the tubes.

Hysterectomy is not ordinarily considered as birth control. It is usually performed in order to correct some female disorder rather than to prevent pregnancy. But since it does involve removal of the womb, which houses the unborn child, hysterectomy does render a woman incapable of reproduction. Removal of the ovaries is usually prompted by medical considerations other than the prevention of pregnancy, but this too renders the woman sterile.

Abortion Abortion, like vasectomy, cutting of the Fallopian tubes, hysterectomy and removal of the ovaries, is a method of birth control. Unlike them, however, abortion does not prevent, but rather interrupts, pregnancy. The union of sperm and egg produces an embryo after which a few weeks is known as a fetus. During the early stages of development it is practically impossible to distinguish the human fetus from that of a fish, a frog or several other life forms. Not until several months after conception does the developing fetus take on features which clearly distinguish it as human. During the first five or six months of the 280-day gestation period, the fetus may be spontaneously or surgically aborted with no funeral being necessary. Prior to approximately the sixth month, the aborted fetus is medically considered and treated as excess body tissue of the mother witn no viable and independent life of its own. If for some reason, all is not well with the fetus or its host environment, nature will cause it to be expelled, thus terminating the pregnancy without producing a birth. Clearly, then, those who argue that at the moment of conception the fertilized egg is simultaneously endowed with a soul, making it human and abortion murder, are on very shaky grounds.

Spontaneous expulsion of the fetus is popularly known as miscarriage. Also during this period the pregnant woman may decide that she cannot or will not continue the pregnancy, and she seeks an abortion. Because most state laws make abortion illegal, many women are forced to become either criminals or hypocrites in order to secure one. Most illegal abortions are preceded by a visit of the woman to a doctor in search of a legal abortion. Since the law makes this practically impossible, except as a direct effort to save the mother's life, she is usually refused. If she is well-to-do, however, the law may be broken to accommodate her. She may be placed in the hospital for "observation" during which time the abortion is performed. Since the law makes this illegal, it is not entered into the records of the hospital, and no reliable estimate of the number of such abortions is possible.

If she cannot get such "legal" help, the woman seeks illegal and sometimes unskilled assistance from one of the hundreds of abortion mills across the country. Estimates from medical sources say that there are between 200,000 and 1,200,000 illegal abortions performed each year in the United States, about 80 percent of them being performed on married women, most of whom already have several children.[11]

Approximately 3 million out of the 25 million married women of child-bearing age in the United States want a child in any one year. This would mean that 22 million are exposed each year to undesired pregnancy. Since the Pill, our most reliable contraceptive, fails for one in every hundred users, and since most women use even less reliable contraceptives, there are 2 to 3 million undesired pregnancies annually among married women.[12]

It is ironic and completely irresponsible for our society to require such careful screening of people who want to adopt children but, at the same time, indiscriminately insist that others go ahead with births they do not want. There are some signs that this societal inconsistency is changing but not necessarily diminishing. The American Medical Association voted in 1967 to change its policy on hospital abortions to permit therapeutic abortions under three conditions: (1) when the pregnancy threatens the life of the mother; (2) when the infant might be born with a disabling physical deformity or mental deficiency; or (3) if the pregnancy results from rape or incest and threatens the mental or physical health of the mother. The AMA position, however, requires documented medical evidence that the abortion is necessary, and two physicians other than the patient's doctor must concur. This is a cumbersome routine and obviously leaves many women without access to the release from pregnancy which they seek.

Shirley S. was attacked and repeatedly raped by a gang of teenage boys. When it was determined that she was pregnant, she and her parents desperately sought an abortion. But because she was young and healthy, and considered emotionally mature by examining psychiatrists, she was denied an abortion. Two weeks later Shirley was dead, killed by an illegal abortionist and archaic ideas.

Until such time as we have a completely effective contraceptive, legal restrictions on abortion make no sense at all. The individual welfare of the mother dictates that she not be sentenced to nine months at hard labor for accidental conception. The collective welfare of our nation makes it imperative that we not inflict upon it children who have no place in the home or in the larger society.

One of the strongest arguments for reform or outright repeal of abortion laws comes from those who cite the health hazard resulting from strict abortion laws. Though abortion performed by a competent physician in a standard hospital has a lower mortality rate than pregnancy and childbirth, it is estimated that criminal abortions cause one fifth of all maternal deaths in the United States.[13] In South America, induced (and illegal) abortions are the Number One cause of female death in women of child-bearing age. The same is true in the Moslem countries which have strict prohibitions against abortions.[14]

Slum and suburban women in the United States use hat pins, coat hangers, putrid soap solutions and unsafe chemical concoctions in efforts to abort themselves. Others intentionally fall down stairs, slip in the bathtub, exercise vigorously, wear tight clothing, assume grotesque positions and even mutilate their bodies—all in a desperate effort to terminate unwanted and unacceptable pregnancy.

In 1968 and 1969 abortion law reform was undertaken in a number of states and, as of mid-1970, a dozen states had amended their laws to permit abortion when the mental health of the mother is endangered or when the pregnancy results from rape or incest. New York State made it possible for any woman over 21 to secure an abortion simply by asking for it. Her request does not have to be approved by a panel of doctors, as some states require. Neither does the woman have to be a resident of New York. Other states which have liberalized (but not abolished) their abortion statutes include Arkansas, California, Colorado, Delaware, Georgia, Hawaii, Kansas, New Mexico, North Carolina, Maryland and Oregon.

On November 10, 1969, Judge Gerhard A. Gesell, of the United States District Court of Columbia, declared unconstitutional a 1901 law which provided for prosecution of physicians who performed abortions in the District. Judge Gesell said that the law was not exact and put undue pressure on physicians, making it impossible for them to provide adequate health care for their patients. The ruling leaves the question of abortion in the District up to the doctor and his patient without legal restrictions. It still bans abortions performed by nonphysicians.

A large number of abortion-law opponents want to repeal rather than to reform existing statutes. Arguing that the law has no just or necessary application to the question, those who push for repeal contend that abortion should be available on demand. So heated and so widespread is the concern with the abortion question, it's surprising to realize that it did not become a national issue until 1962. In that year, Mrs. Robert Finkbine searched the world over for a legal abortion after having taken thalidomide, a new and supposedly safe drug which subsequently caused malformation of more than 10,000 babies in Europe. This new drug had been distributed in Europe to thousands of women in early stages of pregnancy, and Mrs. Finkbine was one of several American women who had received it. She sought help from scores of hospitals and countless doctors without success. Her searches were publicized and millions of Americans for the first time realized the dilemmas posed by our abortion laws.[15]

Another episode in the sixties heightened the issue. The 1963 German Measles epidemic in the United States affected 82,000 women in the first three months of pregnancy. Thirty thousand infants were born dead or died in early infancy. More than 20,000 suffered major abnormalities such as blindness, deafness, heart disease and severe mental retardation.[16]

Because it seeks to remedy a condition which need not have occurred, abortion is a relatively inefficient birth control technique. Were it not for the primitive level of our contraceptive technology, it would be unnecessary for us to be concerned with abortion, except in cases of possible damage to a fetus or danger to the prospective mother. For these two reasons abortion will always be a necessity, but once contraception is sufficiently developed, it will be considerably less needed and less used.

TYPES OF CONTRACEPTIVES

As mentioned earlier all present methods of contraception may be divided into three basic types: biological, mechanical and chemical. The biological method requires no special equipment nor great amount of knowledge on the part of practitioners. Two of the three most commonly practiced forms of biological contraception—abstention from coitus and coitus interruptus—require only super-human will-power and consistent use. Abstention, if practiced over a lifetime, is certainly an effective agent of birth control. But it can be used only by the religious and ascetic few, and certainly has no place in marriage. In fact, failure to consummate a marriage, which means not having sexual relations, is grounds for divorce in many states. Man cannot live without sex any more than he can live without food. Both conditions are fatal if widely practiced and long continued.

Biological Coitus interruptus simply means that the penis is withdrawn while erect and before ejaculation, the result being that the sperm is not deposited in the vagina. If done in time, coitus interruptus will allow sexual intercourse yet prevent conception. This method is thousands of years old and no doubt has resulted in untold millions of unplanned pregnancies. For one thing, it is impossible for the man to know the exact instant when withdrawal is necessary. He who hesitates here is certainly lost because it takes only one of the millions of sperm released during each act of intercourse to impregnate the woman. And some sperm are often released before orgasm or climax, when the male would ordinarily withdraw.

The third biological method of contraception is rhythm, which means adapting sexual intercourse to the woman's menstrual cycle in such a manner as to avoid impregnation. Labeled by critics as Vatican roulette, rhythm is only slightly more effective than nothing. Requiring the careful recording of basal temperature over a prolonged period, rhythm should be recommended only for those with an engineering approach to their sex life and a complete lack of emotional spontaneity. Besides failing more often than succeeding, rhythm requires the presence of elaborate toilet facilities, a great deal of privacy, an inordinate amount of time, proficient record-keeping and an average and healthy body.

The temperature of most women varies little from day to day. There is a rise in temperature, however, associated with the onset of menstruation. By observing those temperature patterns over a few weeks, it is theoretically possible to determine the "safe" period. A woman can conceive for only 24 to 48 hours per month immediately following release of the egg by the ovary. Rhythm advocates contend that by adding several days on either side of this event, and refraining from intercourse during this period, pregnancy can be avoided. Should the woman's temperature vary, however, due to illness or infection or should she simply be subject, as some are, to unexplained and irregular temperature variations, rhythm is impossible. Should her menstrual cycle be irregular, as many are, it becomes absurd even to consider it.

Those who practice rhythm must live in anxious anticipation of the wife's next menstrual period, with a one- or two-day delay being enough to produce panic and accusations from each that it's the other's fault. Such a situation certainly places an intolerable strain on the marriage and does little to alleviate society's problem of too many people.

Mechanical Contraceptives Mechanical methods of contraception employ a device of some sort to prevent the union of sperm and egg. The major mechanical contraceptives include the condom, the diaphragm and the intrauterine device. The condom, the only male contraceptive available, is made either from very thin rubber or the intestines of animals and is shaped like the finger of a glove. It is designed to fit over the erect penis in order to catch the sperm released by the male during sexual intercourse. Approximately 700,000,000 condoms are manufactured annually in the United States for domestic use, which averages about 11 to 13 for each man.[17]

Nothing is more familiar to the American male than the condom dispenser on the wall of public restrooms. Seven-year-old Teddie had again asked his father the same question which always accompanied their stops at the service station, "What's that, Daddy?" As most parents, his father had always managed either to avoid or redirect the question. But now he knew he would never escape until he satisfied his son's inquisitiveness. "That's a machine that sells containers that fit over a penis." With the innocence of a child and the timing of a stand-up comedian, little Teddie asked, "How do you get your penis way up there?"

The principle of the condom has been known since ancient times, and its use is recorded in medical and folk literature of early societies. The word "condom," however, was not included in Webster's Dictionary until the latest edition, an omission symbolic of our backwardness in all things sexual.

If properly and consistently used, the condom is a highly effective means of birth control, but that's a big if. Until 1938 when the Food and Drug Administration began to supervise the manufacture of condoms, the quality was poor and the failure rate was high. Even a tiny hole in the condom can sabotage its purpose. The reliability of the condom in the 1970s depends more on its method of use than its quality, however. All the male must do is to keep a supply constantly available and consistently used. But that is a great deal to expect.

Some men complain that the use of a condom interferes with sexual pleasure and spontaneity. Therefore they either refuse or "forget" to use it. Other men are clumsy in its use, sometimes allowing the condom to slip off during intercourse, spilling semen into the vagina. An unknown but significant proportion of males refuse to use condoms because their sense of masculinity is directly related to the number of times they impregnate a woman. The number of children this man has is a direct reflection of his manliness, and he will do nothing of his own choosing to reduce it.

The major indictment of the condom, though, is the fact that its use is directly tied to the time of coitus. It either interrupts the love-making associated with intercourse or requires that the male anticipate and prepare for each sexual encounter. Even if the technical reliability of the condom were 100 percent, its usage would always be limited by the unpleasant and inconvenient features related to its application.

While the condom prevents entrance of the sperm into the vagina, the diaphragm allows uninterrupted ejaculation to occur. But by covering the entrance to the womb, the diaphragm stops the sperm from entering, thereby preventing conception. Measuring some two to four inches in diameter, the diaphragm is shaped like a shallow cup and is made of soft rubber with a flexible metal spring around the outer edge.

Since sexual anatomy varies from one person to another, the diaphragm must be fitted to each individual woman. The diaphragm is designed to fit between the forward part of the pelvis and the end of the spine. If the fit is not proper, sperm will find their way around the diaphragm and into the womb. In addition to insuring that the diaphragm is of the correct size, the woman who uses it must also position it correctly. Failure at either can be empirically measured nine months later.

For obvious reasons, diaphragms are available only after examination by a doctor and with his written prescription. Since the vagina is stretched at childbirth, periodic refitting of the diaphragm is also necessary. Many women, nurtured on the sexual ignorance and embarrassment of American society, are reluctant to ask a doctor about contraception of any kind, much less one that requires careful and periodic examination of their "private organs." Some of those who have summoned the courage to seek such help from a local physician have learned to their sorrow that a medical degree does not necessarily equip a doctor to prescribe a diaphragm. Dr. Alan Guttmacher, President of Planned Parenthood-World Population, advises women to consult an obstetrician-gynecologist or a general practitioner skilled in contraception.[18] This requirement eliminates the diaphragm as a realistic birth control device for the millions of women who never see such specialists. It also means that the diaphragm could never be more available than the supply of sophisticated medical assistance.

Intrauterine contraceptive devices, first introduced in the United States in 1962, are small metallic or plastic objects placed in the uterus to prevent conception.[19] Though it is not known exactly how the IUD works, it has been found to be an effective means of birth control. IUDs are manufactured in various shapes and of several different materials: plastic spirals, loops and bows, stainless steel, and nylon rings. Unlike the diaphragm, the intrauterine device does not have to be fitted to the woman. It is not meant to act as a barrier between sperm and egg, but to prevent the fertilized ovum from implanting itself in the wall of the uterus where it develops into a fetus. It is thought that the mere presence of this foreign object in the uterus is enough to disturb the hospitality which it customarily offers to the impregnated ovum. Though conception may occur, the IUD does not permit implantation in the uterine wall, and the fertilized egg is discharged in the menstrual flow.

Even though the IUD does not have to be fitted, it should be inserted with medical assistance. The F.D.A. Advisory Committee on Obstetrics and Gynecology reported in the late 1960s that "IUD's are packaged without adequate instruction for use, and many are not marketed in sterile packages with disposable introducers." [20] To avoid possible infection and to assure proper placement, a doctor is needed. Because the uterus is sensitive and damage is possible, the IUD is not recommended for women who have never been pregnant. These liabilities, plus the fact that the IUD can be involuntarily expelled from the uterus, leaving the woman unknowingly unprotected, makes it unlikely that this contraceptive device can ever be effective and reliable enough to support a population control program.

Chemical Contraceptives Some of the mechanical contraceptives are used along with spermicidal chemicals. Many doctors, for example, recommend that the diaphragm be coated with a contraceptive jelly or cream as an extra safeguard. By killing the sperm with which they come in contact, these substances reduce the risk of pregnancy even further.

Tablets, jellies, creams and foams are also used by themselves as contraceptives. Inserted into the vaginal tract shortly before intercourse, these preparations impede the mobility and destroy most or all of the sperm released by the male. Though less effective than mechanical contraceptives alone or mechanical and chemical in combination, these chemicals do somewhat reduce the chances of conception. The major advantage they have is that no prescription is necessary and they are administered by the woman herself. This advantage is offset, though, by the high failure rate of such contraceptives.

The most widely used chemical birth control agent is the oral contraceptive or the Pill. It was in 1955 that Gregory Pincus, an American research biologist, first isolated a group of chemical steroids which would inhibit ovulation when taken orally. He and his associates at the Worcester Institute for Experimental Biology experimented with more than a hundred derivatives of estrogen and progesterone and other chemicals. By 1960 an oral contraceptive based on this principle had been developed, tested and authorized by the Food and Drug Administration for general use.[21] These chemicals inhibit ovulation by inducing a pseudo-pregnancy which causes the female sexual physiology to act much as it would if fertilization had actually occurred. The body, in effect, is tricked into thinking that it's pregnant; hence it does not produce the ova, or egg, without which actual pregnancy cannot occur. Because it's somewhat like being pregnant, the Pill produces some of the symptoms of pregnancy in some women—dizziness, nausea, headaches.

Since 1960, the Pill has become the most popular and widely used contraceptive in America. Planned Parenthood estimates that about eight million women, roughly one third of all fertile women in the country, use the oral contraceptive. It's effectiveness when properly taken is about 99 percent. The early pills were designed to be taken for 20 days at which time they were discontinued until the fifth day of menstruation. If a woman failed to take one of her pills or if she incorrectly calculated the length of her menstrual period, she could well find herself pregnant. Some women have even stopped taking the Pill because of their overwhelming fear that they would do something wrong and be blamed by their husbands for getting pregnant. One woman explained, "I'd rather we take our chances, and if it happens, we're both to blame." To overcome this drawback, some manufacturers began to package the contraceptive pill in a full month's supply. The extra pills were different in color and were placebos, or sugar pills, designed to be taken during the last 10 days of the month. Because the various brands of oral contraceptives contain different combinations of chemicals, primarily estrogen and progesterone which the female body produces naturally, a doctor's prescription is necessary in order to purchase them. Not all contraceptive pills can be taken by all women. For a number of reasons, doctors recommend that women return for a new prescription once a year. Body chemistry may change slightly, making it necessary to change the chemical content of the contraceptive being taken. Adminstration of the same drug over too long a period may cause problems which could be avoided by periodic changes in the amount and type of drug being taken.

At present the Pill is the most effective contraceptive available. However, the Pill requires the individual user to be highly enough motivated to seek a medical prescription and to follow directions for its use over a long period of time. On both counts the Pill is unacceptable as a means for achieving control of population size. In fact, the Pill is a very middle-class contraceptive fit only to enable the affluent to space and limit their procreation. Ruth Henderson lives with her husband on a subsistence farm in the most rural part of the Midwest. Mrs. Parra lives not far from the Alamo in the heart of San Antonio, Texas. Eons of distance, in the first case physical, in the second, social, separate these women from the contraceptive protection to which they are entitled. Contraception for the billions can never be accomplished by a technique which requires such prolonged availability of physicians, such close proximity and regular use of drug stores and such consistent application over a 20- to 30-year period.[22]

During the late sixties and early seventies serious questions emerged concerning the safety of the Pill.[23] Some medical researchers and physicians had been saying for a decade that the FDA acted too hastily in authorizing use of the oral contraceptive. They pointed out that no one knew what the effect would be on women of 20 years' use of the Pill. They raised the spectre of genetic damage to future generations and medical complications for present-day mothers.

Being primarily concerned with the individual health problems of their patients, these medical people advised extreme caution and a go-slow approach to the oral contraceptive. Other segments of the medical profession, viewing the real and present dangers to the health and welfare of our country and our world, tended to put the social good ahead of the individual good. Obviously, they pointed out, no one could know what effect 20 years' use of the Pill might have on women, but we could predict what effect 20 more years of rapid population growth would have on all of us. They also wondered what those who talked about such prolonged experimentation would suggest. Since it is not possible to experiment on human beings, the only way to find out what effect the Pill would have on people was to perfect it on monkeys, rabbits, rats and other laboratory animals; then to use it for people. It was also pointed out that few if any women would actually take the same contraceptive medication for 20 years, since changes and improvement would constantly be made in response to effects of the Pill on earlier users.

In 1970, headlines appeared across the United States announcing, " 'Pill' Labeled Health Hazard," "Contraceptive Linked to Cancer, Blood Clotting," "The Pill: Timebomb or Social Boon," "Doctors Refuse to Recommend Pill." These scare tactics were blamed by some for a drop in the use of oral contraceptives and an anticipated rise in the number of births during the next year. The headlines grew out of studies, primarily in England, showing that women who used the Pill had a higher incidence of pulmonary emboli and cerebral thrombosis (both due to blood clotting) than nonusers. For women users age 20 to 35, the death rate from these two causes was reported to be .5 deaths per 100,000 women each year. For nonusers, the rate was 0.2 deaths for 100,000. In women 35 to 45, the user's rate was 3.9 per 100,000 or one in 25,000 compared to 0.5 for nonusers.[24] The fact that the rate for older women users is considerably higher than that for young users could be related to the fact that the older women have taken the Pill for a longer period of time. On the other hand, it might simply reflect the naturally higher incidence of such diseases among older women. Be that as it may, however, the fact remains that users of all ages have a higher death rate from certain diseases than nonusers. This seems to be related to the tendency of users to develop blood clots which damage either the lungs or the brain.

Approximately 6 out of 100 American women develop breast cancer at some time in their lives. Despite medical advances in diagnosing and treating the disease, the death rate has not improved much over the past two generations. Some researchers have linked breast cancer to use of the Pill, contending that women who use it are more likely to develop cancer than nonusers.

During early 1970, Congressional hearings were held on the safety of the Pill. The testimony was contradictory and sometimes heated, serving more to point up a lack of knowledge than a danger to health. But when all is said and done, perhaps ignorance is the biggest danger of all. At least that seems to have been the public reaction to the hearings. A Gallup Poll conducted shortly afterwards found that American women, by a two to one margin, felt that the Pill was unsafe. The percentage of women who said the Pill was safe declined from 45% in 1967 to 22% in 1970.[25]

Following these hearings, the federal government ordered a warning to be inserted in packages of oral contraceptives. The warning is approximately 100 words long and is a toned-down and shortened version of the 600-word statement originally prepared.[26]

The warning reads:

> The oral contraceptives are powerful, effective drugs. Do not take these drugs without your doctor's continued supervision. As with all effective drugs, they may cause side effects in some cases and should not be taken at all by some. Rare instances of abnormal blood clotting are the most important known complication of the oral contraceptives. These points were discussed with you when you chose this method of contraception.
>
> While you are taking this drug, you should have periodic examinations at intervals set by your doctor. Tell your doctor if you notice any of the following:
>
> 1. Severe headache
> 2. Blurred vision
> 3. Pain in the legs
> 4. Pain in the chest or unexplained cough
> 5. Irregular or missed periods

It is tragic that some women have allowed themselves to be stampeded by over-stated headlines and over-zealous opponents of the Pill.[27] For the sake of argument, let us grant that the higher death rate of pill users is related to its use and not to some as yet undiscovered "other" factor. Though the number of experiments conducted have not been sufficient to document this relationship beyond a reasonable doubt, it probably is true. For no drug is without side effects. Aspirin has been known to kill, and Alan Guttmacher, M.D. says the risk from penicillin is probably higher than from the oral contraceptive.[28] Without question the death rate from pregnancy and childbirth is many times higher than from contraceptives. The sad fact is that America has no "safe" contraceptive, if by "safe" we mean without undesirable and uncontrollable side effects. In large part, this is due to our unwillingness in the past to fund and support contraceptive research and development on anything remotely resembling parity with our other medical technology. It has always been the last to be funded (when it was funded at all), the least funded and the first to be cut. Compared to our medical gadgetry for prolonging life, our contraceptive devices are stone-age medicine, reminiscent more of folk remedies hawked by a traveling con-man than of sophisticated treatments issued from the laboratory and pushed by the medical establishment.

But perhaps the completely safe contraceptive is a goal never to be realized. It may be that we have to accept some personal health risks in order to dampen the threat to our collective existence occasioned by our inclination to breed ourselves into oblivion. If, then, the effectiveness of contraception in controlling ruinous population growth can be demonstrated, we will simply have to accept the risks of contraception as part of the inevitable consequences of having overcome those more immediate risks to which our ancestors were exposed.

How effective are present contraceptives in preventing pregnancy and maintaining desired family and societal size? The answer is, not very effective. Robert Potter, Jr. and James Sakoda developed a mathematical model of fertility data applied to the typical American family, including age at marriage, number of children wanted, type of contraceptive used, and so forth. Using this model, J. F. Hulka, M.D. of the Department of Obstetrics and Gynecology, University of North Carolina School of Medicine, points up the sorry state of our contraceptive development. He found that if 100 couples (after reaching their desired family size of three) used a contraceptive which was 95 percent effective (such as the diaphragm or condom) more than 80 of them would have additional children during their remaining 12 to 15 years of fertile marriage. Three to six of the couples would end up with seven children. Using a 99 percent effective method, such as the Pill and perhaps the IUD, approximately 30 of these couples would wind up with more children than they planned.[29]

Hulka concludes by saying "these calculations are very persuasive toward favoring voluntary sterilization at some point after the family is considered complete, at least until better contraceptives come along."[30]

The case of Ralph and Barbara illustrates our contraceptive primitiveness. Ralph and Barbara are in their late twenties. They have been married for six years and have three children. Barb's first pregnancy was unplanned but not too unwelcome, though Ralph had used a condom most of the time. After the birth, Barb had a diaphragm prescribed by the doctor who delivered the baby. She tried to use it regularly and correctly, but it didn't always work out that way. Thus came the second child. This time she had an IUD inserted. She didn't know until she was pregnant again that it had been expelled. Now Ralph has had a vasectomy and Barb is on the Pill. They explain, "We haven't found anything yet that works, and we're scared to death."

FUTURE CONTRACEPTIVE DEVELOPMENTS

If a policy of compulsory birth control such as I envision is to become a humane reality, it will necessarily be based on a contraceptive which is safer and more effective than any now in use. Fortunately, these new contraceptives are now under study and a number are being tested on experimental animals. Scientists have found several substances which stop the production of sperm when injected into men.[31]

One approach that seems promising is the implantation of a capsule containing a synthetic male hormone which prevents sperm formation. Scientists already know how to construct such capsules so that only tiny amounts of hormone leak continuously into the body. The capsule would provide long-term sterility, and the process is reversible simply by removing the capsule. This type of contraceptive is made possible by constructing capsules out of a type of medical plastic, which is then implanted just under the loose skin at some appropriate place on the body. Halting sperm production, however, eventually results in a reduction of the size of the testes. Although the sex drive is not affected, it is unlikely that a drug with this side effect will ever be accepted.

It is not necessary, though, that a male contraceptive stop the production of sperm. So long as the sperm does not reach the female ova, conception will not occur. Some radical improvement which would make it possible to block the vas deferens, yet unplug it when needed, would fill the bill. It is unlikely that the valve discussed earlier will be sufficient, though some future refinement of it could play a significant part in the population battle. If a process could be developed which would allow the production of sperm yet cause it to be infertile, this might be the major breakthrough needed for a reliable and acceptable male contraceptive. At least one company is presently experimenting with a male oral contraceptive which operates on this principle, and it has been found to be highly effective in laboratory animals. The contraceptive pill for men may be only four or five years away, depending upon the level of funding and political attractiveness.

The future pill for both men and women will bear little resemblance to that now available. Much longer protection will be afforded by a single pill. Periods from one year to twenty years have been mentioned as realistic possibilities by the end of the seventies. This long-term protection would be particularly attractive for couples in their late twenties or early thirties who wanted no more children. Of course, some antidote to restore fertility would be needed if such long-term contraceptives are to be very widely used. Otherwise, the long-term oral contraceptive would suffer the same liability as vasectomy does currently: its irreversibility.

All oral contraceptives now in use are designed to be taken before coitus and the possibility of conception. Experimentally, however, an oral contraceptive, popularly called "the morning-after pill," has been shown to prevent pregnancy. To be taken after intercourse, rather than before, this contraceptive is designed to abort a conception which has already occurred. The woman who takes the pill, of course, never knows if she was actually pregnant. All she knows is that she was exposed to the risk of pregnancy, and the contraceptive removes the risk after rather than before sexual contact.

Such a contraceptive as this offers several advantages over present types. For one thing, it does not have to be taken regularly, but only after each act of sexual intercourse. Its use requires no anticipation or planning other than simply having it available when needed. A second advantage is that for those who find current abortion techniques unacceptable, applied as they are only after the pregnancy is discovered, the morning-after pill prevents not only the pregnancy but the knowledge of it.

A new chemical contraceptive which hopefully will provide protection for a year or more while eliminating the side effects of present oral contraceptives is being tested. It is a hormone contained in a slow-release capsule that is inserted into the womb. The hormone alters the womb lining so that a fertilized egg won't be produced. This contraceptive has been tested successfully but it has not been approved by the Food and Drug Administration as yet. Its benefits include the elimination of blood clots, high blood pressure, headaches and other side effects associated with the present pill.[32]

If pregnancy prevention is viewed in the same way as the prevention of smallpox and polio, then a much better contraceptive is absolutely essential. Alan Guttmacher's *Babies by Choice or by Chance* says:

> It must be foolproof, infallible. It must be cheap. It must be harmless even when used over protracted periods. It must be readily reversible, so that when it is discontinued, fertility will be restored rapidly. It must be simple to apply, requiring neither intelli-

> gence, nor consistently maintained motivation nor special equipment. Finally, its application must be wholly dissociated from the time of coitus.[33]

This ideal contraceptive will be difficult, if not impossible, to develop. Carl Djerassi, professor of Chemistry at Stanford University, argues that FDA standards for contraceptives are unrealistically high and more rigid than those applied to other drugs. He points up the paradox in Western nations, which allows unrestricted sale of tobacco and alcohol, both of which have serious side effects and no socially redeeming qualities (such as birth control), yet insists that contraceptives meet unreasonably high standards of health and safety. Requiring that contraceptives be completely free of side effects and approving them for use only after years of clinical experience, result in too few contraceptives and too many people. Djerassi says, "My thesis is that we cannot afford the luxury of such rigorous standards, which are probably unrealizable . . . and unrealistic . . . . , unless we are prepared to accept the reality that no new birth control agent that meets these standards will ever be developed." [34] Djerassi predicts that fewer drug companies will enter the contraceptive market, and those now in will do less research, all because FDA restrictions are making research more complicated and expensive.

Thus it appears that while the need for a better contraceptive is becoming more urgent by the hour, the likelihood of its development grows ever less, due primarily to our lack of social and political commitment rather than to a lack of technical sophistication. America is the only nation in the world with the scientific competence and financial resources sufficient to develop the ideal contraceptive. For this reason, Djerassi contends that the United States holds the key to the world's population problem. This country must recognize that its virtual scientific monopoly in the field of reproductive physiology imposes upon it a moral and logical obligation to take a global rather than a parochial view of novel contraceptive approaches. The pivotal role for future developments anywhere in the world rests to a considerable extent on government agencies such as the U.S. Food and Drug Administration.[35]

Yet Dr. John Rock, who helped develop the present oral contraceptive, testified before a Senate Committee in December 1969, that "the state of contraceptive technology today is a disgrace to science." Before that same committee, Dr. Joseph W. Goldzieher, Director of the Division of Clinical Sciences of the Southwest Foundation for Research and Education, labeled current contraceptives as "Stone-Age Medicine." [36] Cave-man techniques belong in a museum, not in our legislatures and laboratories.

If compulsory birth control is to become a humane alternative to our present inhuman policies of compulsory crowding and compulsory waste; if birth control is to take its rightful place as the logical foundation for all programs of preventive medicine; if families are to escape the cruel and capricious failures of our present birth control technology, finally, if man is to be the victor rather than the victim, an ideal contraceptive is an absolute necessity.

9 The Purpose of Sex

Be fruitful and multiply and replenish the earth.

—The Old Testament

Wives, submit yourselves unto your husband.

—The New Testament

Sex is fun.

—The New Morality

Perhaps our biggest problem as Americans in dealing realistically with birth control is that sex is involved. And never was a subject better calculated to bring out the worst in us. Our worldwide reputation as practical and hard-headed people could never be applied to our treatment of sex. The traditional American perspective views sex as evil and shames us for expressing sexual desire. Why we don't view hunger and thirst the same way is a question that never occurs to some of us.

The young child discovers his genital organs and he is amazed and delighted. He observes that he is different from his sister. He recognizes that he is like his father and that his sister is like his mother. He has discovered that the world is divided into boys and girls and he knows which he is. The young child takes great delight in discussing his bowel movements and likes to observe both his own body and that of his parents and other children.

To the child, the human body is a thing of beauty and a source of pleasure. The child begins to ask questions. A boy asks, "Mommie, why don't I look like sister?" Or a daughter says, "Daddy, how come I'm not like you?" So begins the process of sex education—certainly a vital part of the child's education, but without a doubt, the area where adults do the poorest job.

A big part of the problem is that we adults have such unhealthy attitudes toward sex. To us sex is simply an act to be committed in secret and discussed in private. Sex is only an inescapable urge designed for reproduction. It is vulgar and dirty, having no virtue or dignity. We fail to recognize that human sexuality has been the inspiration for some of our most beautiful literature, music and art. Around the fact of sex a man and a woman build a marriage and a family. Sex becomes so interwoven with the expression of affection, with love and with mental health, so much a part of our emotional and spiritual states, so meaningful a part of our lives, that we do ourselves and our children a grave disservice by communicating a vulgar or sordid picture of the fundamental fact of life—the fact of human sexuality.

A child first asks questions regarding sex as casually as he asks when dinner will be ready. In most cases, however, the answers he gets so dismay him that his questions become more and more infrequent and his parents' anxiety becomes ever greater. For example, the child asks, "Where did I come from?" Now what do we do? Do we sit down and explain the reproductive process in detail or do we say, "The stork brought you." Or do we say "Ask your father"—or "mother," as the case may be. How do we know what the child really wants to know? Johnny asked his mother one day, "Where did I come from?" This was the moment she had dreaded for so long. She searched her mind frantically for an answer. She couldn't decide which course to take, so she asked, "Why do you want to know?" Johnny said, "I just wondered, Jimmy Jones says he came from Chicago."

A child's questions should be treated just for what they are—a child's questions. They deserve an honest answer, one which he can understand and which does not raise a multitude of other questions. The child asks, "Where do babies come from?" He won't understand chromosomes and genes and zygotes and fetus, but he will understand, "A seed from Daddy joined an egg in Mother and you grew inside her." From what he is told and the way he is told, the child will develop a life-long attitude toward sex.

Parents, then, should be prepared to discuss sex with their child. In order to do this, however, parents must first understand the importance of sex for life in general and for themselves in particular. The tragedy of American sex is that few of us know the facts of human sexual anatomy and physiology and even fewer have worked out the sexual philosophy by which we live. With respect to sex and the education of our children, adults can be placed in two categories: those who tell too little and those who tell too much. The first group has grown up sexually ignorant and can only perpetuate that condition in their children. Even though they have participated in the reproductive process, they do not know how it works and cannot explain their attitude toward it. The second group has a finely honed verbal facility perfected by term papers and scholarly discipline. They know all the words and are familiar with all the philosophies of life and sex. They are proud of their learning and eager to demonstrate their sophistication. Yet when dealing with children, most of them tell more than the youngsters want to know. These adults hide the fact that they really don't know what they're talking about by never allowing the questioner time enough to think about what he has been told. The child is overwhelmed with such a flood of words that even he may not realize for a time just how little he has learned.

The fact that "sex education" in public schools is such a

hotly debated issue all across the United States is proof of our ignorance. The first group of parents described above are against sex education, as they are against new math, new morality, new everything—because it makes them feel uncomfortable. They never had it and they don't see why their children should. They accuse proponents of sex education of being communist, atheist, subversive, and any other unpopular name that's handy. They claim its their right to teach their children "the facts of life," though most of them never intend to exercise that right. "Sophisticated" parents on the other hand, grant a blanket endorsement to sex education as they do to all things new. They seem to fear that their membership in the "now generation" might be withdrawn if they were to question any idea or action labeled "progressive." Neither group does any thinking; they only react as they have been conditioned to certain trigger words: conservative, liberal, progressive, reactionary, etc.

I am opposed to sex education. I am also opposed to stomach education and to brain education. I am for human education which relates all that man is to all that he might be. Except for the specialist who needs to know the subtleties of various parts of the human anatomy, the rest of us need to integrate man's diverse parts and functions into an understanding of the totality of human life. We cannot understand man by studying his parts, for he is more than the sum of those parts. To understand sex in human life, we must be acquainted with all that a human being is and does. "Sex education" distorts sex by separating it from the rest of life, giving the impression either that sex is more of life than it really is or that it is simply knowing names and recognizing anatomy. Sex education localizes sex and equates it with the genitals. It fails to stress the diversity of outlooks and the difference in life styles associated with masculinity and femininity. Sex education does not provide the learner with an appreciation for the emotional, the aesthetic, the political, the mental characteristics related to sex, out of which comes the frustrating, exhilarating, challenging ambivalence of the man-woman relationship. If we were as sophisticated in the space program as in sex education, the Wright Brothers would today be written off as communist agitators for suggesting that man change his traditional mode of travel.

American adults talk and think of superficial sexiness rather than fundamental sexuality. We worship as sex goddesses those females with seductive voices and overly developed mammary glands. Though they may be as cold as a well-digger's knee, completely devoid of human warmth and compassion, they have the shape and the moves which we call sexy. Topless waitresses, plunging necklines, mini-skirts, swivel hips, go-go dancers, nude theatre, Playboy bunnies, call girls, wife swapping, serial polygamy—these are only the more obvious manifestations of our sexy society. American sex is statistically measured: 36–24–36. But these are the signs of a superficial and unstable accommodation to sex. It is a pseudo-sophistication which substitutes exposure for explanation. Vance Packard has correctly labeled America *The Sexual Wilderness*.[1] Sex in America is exhibited and exploited, commercialized and computerized, hated and hunted. Seldom is it understood or appreciated.

The Church has been primarily responsible for originating and spreading the distorted view of sex underlying our present difficulties. Taking its cue from Paul and St. Augustine, the Church taught that it was desirable to abstain from sexual intercourse in order to attain a more religious existence. Recognizing, however, that most men were weak (and therefore religiously inferior) and that the race must be propagated, permission was reluctantly granted for sexual relations—but only for procreation. If one felt any pleasure from sexual union, he was to seek God's forgiveness of his lustful nature.

The Church Fathers of the Middle Ages approved of marriage, but only because it substituted for a worse evil, that of fornication (premarital sexual relations). St. Jerome recognized the superiority of virginity over marriage when he advised a young girl who had taken a vow of viriginity: "Do not court the company of married ladies . . . Learn in this a holy pride: know that you are better than they." [2] Early theology and philosophy were repelled by human sexuality and would have denied its expression, and probably its existence, if it could have prevailed upon the Creator to devise another method.

Modern physiology and psychology are teaching us, though, what we should have known all along. Just as hunger is more than filling the belly, so sex is more than producing offspring. Almost any food will satisfy hunger and that food may be eaten with gluttonous abandon. But under proper conditions, hunger produces an aesthetic experience combining music, lighting, color, taste, texture, conversation, and in the process an elemental human drive acquires elegance, excitement and a more profound meaning.

So with sex. Given the proper setting, sexual union between a man and woman in marriage serves to create in both a sense of oneness with each other and with life. It elevates tenderness to a level not otherwise known to either of them. Sexual intercourse thus seen becomes an expression of love and serves to perpetually remind both husband and wife of the past they have shared and the future they anticipate.

This ideal sexual union between man and woman can be attained, however, only if the expressive and procreative functions of sex can be separated. If the couple—or either of them alone—must be concerned about an unwanted pregnancy, then their relationship will never approximate the ideal. If the wife is chronically tired because of too many children, and the husband is anxious about mounting debt, both their marital relationship and their parental role will be destroyed. Far from elevating man's animal nature, birth control heightens his humanity and rends order from chaos.

THE TECHNOLOGY OF SEX

Man has been chained for most of his existence to a view of sex as being only for procreation. Since the sexual drive compelled male and female together, and since this togetherness inevitably produced children, it was reasonable that the procreative aspects of sex should be stressed to the virtual exclusion of all else. Rules were carefully worked out and passed from one generation to another dictating who was to have sexual access to whom and under what conditions.

For example, all state laws require a minimum age for marriage. No marriage is permitted in some states for "imbeciles, epileptics, persons of unsound mind or persons under the influence of liquors or narcotics. No marriage for those afflicted with a transmissible disease." [Does this include a cold?] "Idiots and lunatics may not marry." "Man may not marry mother, daughter, granddaughter, sister, half-sister, aunt, half-aunt, niece, half-niece, father's widow, son's widow, stepdaughter, wife's granddaughter." [3]

In Western society these and other regulations prohibited sexual relations before marriage and outside marriage, the purpose being to ensure that children were born into an established family equipped to meet their physical and emotional needs. Sex was defined as an inescapable but animal urge on the part of the husband to which the wife's duty was submission. Sex was more an ordeal, tolerated by necessity as release of male tensions and for continuation of the species. Sex was purely survival, both of the man-woman relationship and life itself. In this context, the Western philosophy of sex was developed. It was perfected in the Puritan sexual ethics of early America where adultery was punished by branding an "A" on the forehead, and "sinful dalliance" as premarital sexual relations were called, resulted in public floggings. If the premarital activity were discovered years after its occurrence, even though the two were then married to each other, the public flogging and ridicule were still administered.

The reason sexual contact outside of marriage was so severely treated was that pregnancy and childbirth were likely to result. It was not really the *fact* of sexual intercourse which lay behind all the prohibitions against it, but the likelihood of conception. Over the last century or two, Western man has increasingly intervened in his own evolution. Many of the operations of nature have been described and modified as technology has been applied to them. Such has been the case with sex. Contraceptive technology has made it possible to separate sexual intercourse from conception, making it possible (and necessary) for us to rethink the philosophy of sex worked out before contraception. A very simple formula can be stated:

$$\text{coitus} - \text{contraception} = \text{procreation}$$
$$\text{coitus} + \text{contraception} = \text{expression}$$

Obviously, it is impossible without contraception to think of sex as anything other than procreation. If each time male and female are joined in sexual union the creation of a new life is an unavoidable possibility, both the frequency of such union and its emotional context will be determined. On the other hand, if the possibility of conception can be reduced or eliminated, sex becomes an entirely different matter. For the woman on the Pill, sexual submission as a duty no longer can be justified. She has been emancipated. She can express her sexuality as she expresses her opinion—because of the meaning it has for her as an individual. The man who has had a vasectomy performed cannot think of his sexual life in terms of fatherhood and family. He can no longer psychologically or physically coerce his wife into sexual submission by appeal to her duty and responsibility.

Sex becomes, at least potentially, a mutually satisfying relationship between man and woman, serving to express their affection and need for each other. The purpose of sex is as much social and psychological as it is physical. Contraception allows more equal emphasis upon all three, making for a more enjoyable and healthier relationship.

Some people argue that contraception is inherently immoral. Others contend that it could be used for immoral purposes. The first is wrong. The second is right.

Those who argue that contraception is immoral make statements such as: "It's not natural to interfere with the process of conception." "Man is playing God." "If God hadn't meant man and woman to reproduce, He would have made them sterile."

Suppose we grant the argument that it is not natural to interfere with conception. We would have to admit also that organ transplants and air conditioning, jet planes and television, astronauts and automobiles are equally unnatural. But on the other hand, how can man do anything that's not natural for man to do? If he does it, it's natural.

The problem arises because the word, "natural," is used with two different meanings. One meaning refers to the fact that a thing did not exist in nature prior to man's invention of it. In this sense, contraception and all the rest of human culture is unnatural. But this is obvious and is really no argument at all unless we endorse the elimination of all man-made changes and a complete return to a state of nature.

No critics of contraception go this far. All accept some of the changes man has made as natural. If nothing else, they accept man-made shelter and domesticated plants and animals.

What most critics mean when they object to contraception as unnatural is that it violates their concept of man's relationship to his world. When they say it's not natural, they mean it's not "right" as *they* define right. It will lead to some conclusion or condition which they dislike. It's not so much the thing itself which they deplore but its consequences. Such critics of birth control do not object to the contraceptive itself, but to the presumed undesirable consequences of pregnancy control.

Many today argue that contraceptives for the *unmarried* will destroy their morals. That same argument was used against contraception for the *married* years ago. Describing the attitude in the 1930s, Margaret Sanger wrote:

> The moral question of birth control was at that time constantly debated. Opponents hurled at us the statement that this knowledge would cause immorality among young people; that promiscuity, vice, prostitution would be the inevitable fruits of

> our efforts. This I did not believe. I knew that morality or immorality is not an external factor in human behavior; essentially it grows, emerges, and comes from within. If the young people of the war aftermath were slipping away from the old, moral codes, it was not the fault of birth control knowledge any more than it was the fault of any other progressive or advanced idea of the modern day. Henry Ford's automobiles made transportation available for thousands of young people—morality or immorality as a consequence should not be placed at the door of Mr. Ford.[4]

Some would have us believe that to remove the fear of pregnancy would lead to increased promiscuity. In some cases, no doubt, it would, as did the automobile, the drive-in movie and the motel. But the prevailing opinion among physicians and sociologists is that a girl who is promiscuous on the Pill would have been promiscuous without it. It is unlikely that the mere availability of contraceptives will cause either male or female in great numbers to do what they would not have done otherwise. Obviously some will use contraceptives for sexual exploitation, but it is better for them and for society that pregnancy be avoided. The more mature of the unmarried in this generation say that rather than promoting promiscuity the Pill imposes a sense of responsibility. Now an unmarried girl has to design her sexual life according to her own conscience rather than out of fear of some undesirable social stigma. This same relationship between morality and technology will likely prevail as more efficient contraceptives for both male and female are developed. The benefits of contraception for those who want to use it legitimately and wisely will always outweigh the possibility of its misuse.

The irony of birth control is that it makes sexual behavior more moral, not less. To refrain from sexual activity because of fear of getting caught is not morality but caution. An action is moral only when prompted or hindered by what is right as defined by the individual conscience. What this means is that a new rationale for sexual responsibility and exclusiveness is needed.

THE MINI-MOOD

Victorian prudery shrouded and shriveled sexual development. The body was clothed from head to toe in loose-fitting garments which gave little hint of the anatomy within. Out of sight, out of mind seemed to be the principle by which our ancestors sought to reduce life to a neuter monotony. The human body was taught to be evil and ugly and one was to feel embarrassment at his or her own nakedness. Even in marriage, privacy and secrecy were to separate husband and wife as much as humanly possible.

As a supplement to the sexlessness induced by abundant clothing, our ancestors attempted to frighten young men from premarital and promiscuous sex with horror stories about venereal disease and the unpleasantness of forced marriage. Young women were told of the shame of illegitimacy and the likelihood of pregnancy accompanying the loss of virginity prior to marriage. Like small children warned against lying and stealing by frightening descriptions of hellfire and brimstone, young men and women with normal sexual desires were hounded by visions of syphilitic insanity and social rejection.

The development of contraceptives has largely erased the possibility of frightening adolescents into sexual asceticism. The danger of venereal disease is sharply reduced by use of the condom and penicillin has proved an effective attack on sexually transmitted diseases. The possibility of unintended pregnancy has been reduced (some mistakenly think it has been eliminated), thereby largely removing the threat of discovery and rejection. In the process, contraceptives have pointed up our utter lack of a well-formulated moral base for our sexual philosophy. Much of the current experimentation with sex by the young may be seen, not as a liberation of animal appetites through contraception, but as a reaction against the fear and repression which formerly masqueraded as sexual morality.

The current emphasis on nudity and eroticism in American culture is to be seen as a reaction against the equally ridiculous sexual repression growing out of our Puritan tradition. The mini-mod-mood of the late 1960s and 1970s overemphasizes and exploits sex just as the Victorian-Puritan combine of the 1660s and 1670s underemphasized and exorcised it. If we can keep our wits about us and maintain a sense of perspective and humor, we will work our way through our current difficulties with sex to a more mature and satisfying exercise of our sexual potential.

In large part the question is what we will do with contraception! Will we seize the opportunity to make it an instrument on which we base a carefully thought-out philosophy of sex? Will we realize its contribution to the solution of our population problems? Will contraception free us to solve the ethical and political problems associated with our sexuality, or will it free us only for selfish and shortsighted indulgence of a biological urge?

Fortunately there is some evidence that a humane philosophy of sex is emerging. One well-known Protestant scholar has said:

> Sexual intercourse is an act of the whole self which affects the whole self; it is a personal encounter between man and woman in which each does something to the other, for good or ill, which can never be obliterated. Sex is one of God's gifts to man and woman, and as such, is good in itself, and to be received with thanksgiving; there is no place for the unconsciously blasphemous attitude which regards the right use of sexual activity as something "nasty" or "impure." [5]

If we can grasp this opportunity to devise a sane and sensible sexual philosophy; if we can realize the richness and meaning which come to our lives through our sexuality; if we will adapt our technology to our humanity, rather than the other way around, as we seem ever inclined to do—then we shall find ourselves in a position to solve the personal and social problems associated with sex.

This is a big order, but it is possible. It is not idle and ideal but pragmatic and practical. There will always be those who say a thing is impossible, but such a judgment indicates more about the individual who speaks than the condition he describes. What is possible and practical is determined by our imagination and capacity for hard work. The difficult we do right away, the impossible takes a little longer.

Contraception makes it possible to view sex as voluntary, interpersonal behavior rather than a necessary act of survival. Sex becomes a special method of communication between male and female. Sex thus loses its exclusively biological meaning and becomes more social. Like all social relationships, sex can be made constructive or destructive, depending upon the attitude and behavior of those involved. Sex can become a dialogue between two people in which each comes to understand and appreciate the other. It can be an expression of the mutual dependence so fundamental to human existence. Sex can be an enriching and compassionate human encounter or simply another opportunity for exploitation, satisfying a biological urge but destroying humanity socially and spiritually.

It's up to us.

10 A Population Policy for America

We have met the enemy, and they are us.

—Pogo

Someone has said that we live at the hinge of history. An old world is dying; a new one is painfully being born, and it is not certain that we can survive the transition. Whether we do depends largely upon the kind of decisions we make during the 1970s. For what we decide to do in this decade could very well determine the future of mankind for the next 1,000 years.

Decisions are always difficult to make, but particularly so in time of crisis; paradoxically, it is in time of crisis that decisions are most demanded. How pleasant it would be and how well we could do, we like to think, if only the world would hold still until we could get our bearings. Then we would understand the situation and could make sound decisions.

But such reasoning is deceptive. It is the nature of the human predicament always to have to act on partial knowledge; never do we have full understanding. Anyone who believes he has all the answers simply doesn't understand the situation.

All of us have learned to live with a normal amount of uncertainty and confusion. Events and conditions have conspired, however, to make our age one of those half dozen or so critical periods in human history wherein the whole fabric of society is ripped apart. Centuries of unquestioned assumptions which we thought eternal, have been attacked and abandoned. Institutions that have long served us crumble under the onslaught of new needs and changing values.

The human drama has now reached the point at which a script revision is necessary if a tragic climax is to be averted. If Shakespeare was right when he described the world as a stage on which we are the actors, it follows that someone must supply us with dialogue and action. Depending on the writers we have, we will, as in all good fairy stories, live happily ever after or, as in contemporary literature, die without reason in a world without hope. The American scenario is in progress, but the conclusion has not yet been determined. What will it be? Who will answer?

I have an answer. It's as obvious to me as it is difficult for some. In time of crisis, those things most taken for granted need most to be examined. If we are to solve the many social and personal problems plaguing our society, we must carefully reexamine and redefine parenthood in America. America simply cannot continue its reckless and uncontrolled population growth. If this country had the technology of the seventies and the population of the thirties, our land would make the Garden of Eden seem like a deprived area. But if we add another 100 million people, as demographers anticipate, by the year 2000, the 1970s will, by comparison, be remembered as a paradise.

The control of population size is of the utmost urgency, but we must understand that control is only a means to an end—that end being survival, both of humanity and humanness. I say this because some of those currently recommending population control measures have obviously forgotten it. Their proposals read like a catalogue of horrors. While they might preserve life, they would destroy the reasons for living. To survive, we would have to abandon most of the virtues and values which sustain us.

Some Unreasonable Suggestions

Some suggest that we force wives and mothers to work while at the same time providing few child care facilities. While this would certainly reduce the birth rate, it would also deprive children of necessary care and attention. Those who make such proposals are obviously ignorant of American history. Between the end of the Civil War and the turn of the century, American mothers (and children) were forced to work. Wages were so low and educational opportunities so rare, that parents and children had no choice but to work. Economic and social policies of that period sought only to feed the labor demands of a rapidly industrializing economy, and little provision was made for home life or the development of individual potential.

During the early part of this century, however, America began to realize that its home life had to be strengthened if its people were to realize their personal and social potential. The creation of the Children's Bureau and the Women's Bureau around 1912 served as official recognition of the central place of family life in our national policy. The creation of the public school system and the passage of compulsory attendance laws in the early 1900s helped to make home and school the twin supports of American life.

To provide less care for children by forcing the mother to work while providing no substitute facilities would lead to an increase in juvenile delinquency, mental and emotional trauma, educational problems and a dangerous adulthood. To force women to work would also aggravate employment and economic problems. Whereas two wage earners in a family would perhaps strengthen its financial condition, that second job could be obtained only by denying a first job to another family. Thus we would have a large number of American families in which both husband and wife were employed and another sizeable number in which neither could find work.

In fact, increased unemployment has been proposed as a population control measure. Remembering the Depression when unemployment was high and birth rates were low, this proposal would deprive millions of families of an income in order to force lowered fertility. Such a policy would obviously discriminate against the poor and the less educated and would directly conflict with other social policies designed to reduce poverty and unemployment while increasing the general level of education. Justice will not allow social policies which operate differently on the various segments of our population. For too long we have singled out the poor and the powerless as objects of remedial legislation and social policy. Such a course of action is not only unfair but inefficient. Any significant change in the American social structure, particularly the control of population growth, will occur only when all of us, rich and poor, black and white, Catholic and Protestant, educated and illiterate, are required to change.

Another suggested economic attack on the population problem would encourage migration to the city by offering good jobs at high wages while reducing the number and quality of rural jobs. This proposal is based upon the fact that urban populations have lower birth rates than rural people. Therefore, it is reasoned, once all or nearly all the people are city dwellers, population growth will decline. But what about crime, pollution, taxes, noise, alienation and a host of other undesirable conditions which feed on urban man? Are we to accept these as the price of population control? If so, what will population control have accomplished?

Luring people to the city would increase congestion and would ultimately reduce the birth rate and increase the death rate. Epidemics and contagions would periodically decimate the population. Life expectancy would fall. Social disorganization of every conceivable type would rise. Man would become an animal in an urban jungle, stalked by fear, victimized by his own stupidity. Population growth would no longer be a problem, but humanity would no longer be a possibility.

It has been proposed that the birth rate could be lowered

by making citizens more politically insecure. If we all were subject to arrest and imprisonment, with no rights of appeal; if our homes were invaded by state authorities in the night; if we were deprived of free speech; if insecurity and uncertainty were our constant companions, then the birth rate would certainly fall. Historically, a declining birth rate has served as the passive resistance of a people to a calloused and unpredictable political regime. Fear of the present and uncertainty about the future act as dampers on the birth rate, but they also kill man's spirit. To die spiritually in order to live physically is a fool's bargain, offering only the illusion rather than the substance of living.

Some population control enthusiasts encourage increased homosexuality as a population control measure while others point out that drug addiction and alcoholism also reduce the probability of marriage and parenthood. Others recommend that unmarried women be encouraged to have children, reasoning that single women would have fewer children than married ones. I was taken to task by a woman in the audience for even mentioning the word "marriage" during a panel discussion of population problems. "Marriage is a bourgeois institution," she charged, "built on the exploitation of women. We won't solve any problems until we do away with the family."

If those who point up such "solutions" do so in order to demonstrate the need for drastic action, they certainly accomplish their purpose. If, on the other hand, these are serious proposals, their advocates have completely misjudged the tolerance limits of the American people. We are not about to endorse measures which in themselves are serious personal and social problems. If we can avoid dying of cancer only by committing suicide, what will we have accomplished?

In terms of social characteristics, man is not born human, but becomes so in interaction with his fellows. Obviously, all of us inherit certain physical characteristics which label us as *homo sapiens,* but the shape of a package indicates little of the contents. We have all heard it said of someone, "He's not human," yet none of us would take that statement to mean that the individual being described did not have the essential human anatomy. Rather, we understand such a description to mean that the behavior and actions of the individual are not human—they do not give evidence of the thought processes, the motivations, the sentiments and the objectives which make us human. The human potential moves us to love and to be loved, to help and to be helped. It propels our search for meaning and beauty. It allows brutality but modifies it with conscience. Population control which is achieved at the expense of our humanity is a cure infinitely worse than the disease.

Another suggested birth control method involves treating public water supplies with fertility inhibitors. This would be ineffective for two reasons. First, other life forms would also suffer a reduction in fertility. Of course this would be avoided if the treatment affected only human beings. But all chemical contraceptives now in use affect other life forms. In fact, it has been the availability of experimental animals on which these chemicals could be tested that has made their development possible. Since direct experimentation on human beings is prohibited, any chemical which depressed human fertility alone is difficult to detect and impossible to perfect.

That being the case, the treatment of water supplies to control fertility would be unworkable. Fertility restorers would have to be developed for application to the nonhuman animal and vegetable life essential for human survival. Such an undertaking would make bailing the ocean with a sieve seem like an easy day's work.

A second difficulty has to do with the necessity for reversal in a program designed to inhibit human fertility. I know of no other medical treatment wherein the possibility of its reversal at some future date must be a consideration in the initial application. If we were to treat the water supply with fertility inhibitors, it would be necessary for those in whom fertility was to be restored to secure their drinking water elsewhere. If they continued to drink treated water, they would continue to be infertile. This means that an auxiliary water supply system would have to be developed but its use restricted to those legally entitled to fertility.

It is frequently observed when discussing pregnancy in our usual light-hearted manner, "It's in the water." It would be a mistake if that remark ever were to describe our population policy.

It may be that such drastic proposals will perform a valuable service in the population control dialogue. The fact that they are put forth will, hopefully, move this nation to view compulsory birth control as a more acceptable and effective population policy than it would otherwise. Once the American people realize that our only real alternative is between direct and compulsory control of population size and the indirect and inhuman policies just described, then we can move with the necessary speed and resolve.

It has been suggested that fertility could be controlled through the issuance of marketable licenses to have children. Under this provision couples would be licensed to give birth to a certain number of children, depending upon the need of society and the language of the law. If a couple did not wish to have the number of children to which their license entitled them, they could offer their unwanted fertility for sale to the highest bidder. Such a system as this would result in an invidious discrimination against the poor, for they would be priced out of the market. They would not be financially able to purchase fertility on the open market and it is unlikely that government would subsidize their buying power.

The poor would also be under strong economic pressures to sell rather than to exercise the fertility to which their own permits entitled them. The ready market for their potential children would provide a temporary escape from their poverty. By driving their birth rate down, this system would also enhance the long-range economic outlook for the poor. But the discriminatory features of such a policy make it unworkable and politically unattractive. It would also be inefficient, since affluent Americans contribute most to the pregnancy epidemic.

The conventional wisdom has long recognized that "the rich get richer, and the poor get children." Under a system of marketable fertility licenses, the rich would get both.

Another, seemingly more modest, proposal to attack the population problem has been made by several state and national legislators. Senator Robert Packwood (R-Ore.) introduced a bill in early 1970 to limit income tax exemptions for children to no more than three per family. His proposed legislation, designed to become law in 1973, would allow a $1,000 tax exemption for the first child, $750 for the second, $500 for the third and nothing for additional children.

It is ironic that this proposal has been attacked by some who brand it an anti-motherhood, anti-child doctrine. For the truth of the matter is that the proposal is actually pro-natalist, and if it had any affect at all on the birth rate, it could only be to maintain fertility at a dangerously high level. Under current law, a family with three children is entitled to $1,800 per year in personal income tax exemptions—$600 for each child. Senator Packwood's proposal would actually raise the exemptions for three children from $1,800 to $2,250 per year. In effect, each of the first three children would draw a tax exemption of $750.

This proposed legislation also misses the mark by allowing for the third child. If American families average three children per family, rather than two, over the next five generations—approximately 125 years—the total population would be more than 400 million greater.[1] In response to these considerations, Senator Packwood modified his original bill to allow exemptions for only two natural children.

Suppose there were two families living side by side in 1850. Family "A" has two children and Family "B" has three. If each child in both families has the same number of children as his (her) parents, Family "B" will have 729 children in 1975 while Family "A" will have 64. Let's take a look at how it happens.

The two children in Family "A" in 1850, each have two, for a total of four in 1875. The three children in Family "B"

each have three, for a total of nine. Thereafter, the number in each family grows every 25 years as follows:

Time	Number of Children in Each Family	
	"A"	"B"
1850	2	3
1875	4	9
1900	8	27
1925	16	81
1950	32	243
1975	64	729

If, beginning in 1970 and continuing indefinitely, American women were to have no more than 2.1 children on the average, the population would grow to approximately 295 million (a 44% increase over 1970) by the year 2040 and would thereafter remain constant. If American women average slightly over three children, as they presently do, the total population in 2040 will be some 450 million, a 245% increase over 1970.[2] If American families average just over two children for the next five generations, a maximum population size of 295 million will be attained in the year 2040 and will thereafter remain constant. The three-child family would, over the next five generations, produce a total population of some 600 million people, placing America's size somewhere between present-day India and Mainland China.[3] But this doesn't tell the whole story.

It takes approximately 2.1 to 2.3 children per family to stabilize population size provided that the age distribution of the population is not heavily weighted in favor of the young and provided that death rates are fairly low. In the 1970s, America has the low death rate but it also has a very young population. "In 1970, therefore, America will have a very small group aged 0–4 and considerable groups at ages 5–9, 10–14, 15–19, and 20–24, which will result from the fertility conditions of the 1940s, 1950s and early 1960s."[4]

Because of its young population and its long life expectancy, a completed family size slightly in excess of two children per woman would continue to increase America's population size until near the middle of the twenty-first century. Even a completed family size of exactly two children per family, though too small to replace the parents over a long period of time, would produce an increase in the short run. However, if completed family size were to be no larger than 2.0 rather than 2.1, maximum population size would be attained somewhat earlier than 2040 and would be several million fewer. If after 2040, families were to continue at the level of two children, population size would decline by some 15% to 20% every generation.[5] Thus by the year 2095 the two-child family would have produced a total population of approximately 189 million, smaller than at present.

This reduction would occur because the two children born to each family would not actually replace the two parents over time. Some of the children would die as infants, others would be accidentally killed before reaching adulthood. Some would not have an opportunity to marry, and some would choose to remain single. A few who did marry would not be fertile; others would choose to remain childless. For all these reasons, no more than two births per family would reduce the American population by approximately 20% each generation, whereas the three-child family would continue to increase our already severe population pressures. The difference in five generations (beginning in 1970) between the two-child and the three-child family is better than 400 million people. It is the difference between a population of 189 million and nearly 600 million. Clearly, no policy which seeks to stabilize American family size at three children per family has any possibility for bringing population growth under control. Even two children per family would continue population growth for better than 60 years. The rate of growth, however, would be much slower than at present and would permit us to free much needed resources for application to increasingly serious social problems.

If our goal were to stabilize the size of America's population

at its present level, it would be necessary immediately to limit each family to an average size of 1.2 children for the next two decades. After that time, ". . . the mean number of children per family would have to increase gradually, reaching a maximum of 2.8 children in the period 2030–35." [6]

A 1969 legislative proposal by State Representative Richard Lamm of Colorado would grant tax exemptions to residents of that state for only two natural children plus any number of adopted children. Granting tax exemptions for two children rather than three is a much more sensible proposal for the control of population growth. But all proposals to restrict tax exemptions for children suffer a common liability, for each would fall with a heavier hand upon the poor than upon the affluent. Since the poor have limited access to contraceptives, they are less able to control their fertility. Limiting tax exemptions, would further deprive the poor of funds, thereby decreasing their access to birth control information and technology. Thus would begin the downward spiral of the poor—more kids, less money; less money, more kids, like a monkey chasing its tail, becoming ever more frantic, ever less rational.

I do not think that any of the suggestions discussed above are sufficient weapons against runaway population growth. All of them contain discriminatory provisions which make them unacceptable. Compounding this liability, making all the proposals even less effective, is the fact that the discrimination is directed primarily at those who are least responsible for the problem. Like the jailer who locks up the victim to protect him from the criminal, these proposals restrict the innocent and condone the guilty. Such ill-considered social policies must not be allowed.

America must move toward a population policy aimed at a zero rate of growth. To accomplish this immediately would mean that family size would have to equal approximately 1.2 children. In practical terms, this means that most families would be limited to only one child while some would have two or more. It would be literally impossible, however, given our present state of public suspicion and mistrust, to arrive at any formula for compulsory birth control which would grant greater fertility to one population segment than to another. Even if all of us could agree on such a formula, we have no legitimate basis on which to decide who should get more and who should get less.

Even if America adopts a policy of compulsory birth control, it is very unlikely that we could bring ourselves to restrict parents, even for a decade or so, to only one child. But if we should restrict all parents to a maximum of two children, average completed family size would be reduced to roughly 1.7 or 1.8 children due to the families who either chose to have fewer children or were biologically unable to have two.

America has only two workable alternatives. One is to do nothing, and to let present conditions run their course. This is decision by default and can have no other conclusion than the extinction of mankind. The other alternative is to impose a parenthood ban which applies uniformly to all people. This is decision by design and will ensure the continuation of mankind and the preservation of humanness.

COMPULSORY BIRTH CONTROL

A policy of compulsory birth control is our Number One national priority. It must contain the following minimum provisions:

First, contraceptive advice and materials, including vasectomies and male contraceptives, shall immediately be made available to every American. Current medical practice dictates that vaccine against smallpox, polio and other epidemic diseases must be available to every American. Legislation has also been passed to protect workers against industrial accidents and to protect the public from environmental hazards. The rights of every American are violated by the failure of government to insist that contraceptives be made equally available to all. The civil and personal rights of first-born children are also violated by the birth of later children, ensuring as it does, that all will have less and be less.

But availability of contraceptives is not enough; usage must also be increased. An educational campaign to encourage more extensive and effective use must be mounted. The mass media, schools, churches, parents, the government—all must become more concerned and more competent in regard to contraceptive information and attitudes. The medical profession must begin to exercise the leadership which the public has a right to expect. Opinion makers and community leaders must define adequate contraceptive education as an integral part of their responsibilities.

Secondly, abortion must be legalized and the techniques perfected so as to ensure maximum safety and utilization. The present laws which make abortion a criminal problem should be repealed, and abortion should be recognized for the medical problem which it is. With our present inefficient contraceptives, unplanned and unwanted pregnancies occur by the millions. Both as a population control measure and as freedom from involuntary servitude, abortion must be made more available. Until we can liberalize our policies on abortion, it is unlikely that we can move beyond this issue to the next steps which are needed. It is not that abortion is an efficient, long-term, population control technique. It is not. Once contraceptive technology is sufficiently developed, abortion would be unnecessary except for those few but inevitable contraceptive failures and those diseases of pregnancy which endanger the mother and/or the fetus. Following World War II, the Japanese, by legalizing abortion, cut their birth rate in half in only a decade. After that period, however, they fell back on contraceptives as their front-line defense against population growth.

The more effective distribution of contraceptives and the easier availability of abortion, as necessary as they are, will not achieve population stability. Colorado State Representative Richard Lamm comments:

> Statistics available at present suggest that making complete fertility control available, while the first step, is no more than that—the first step. The demographic effect of removing all restrictions on contraception and abortion probably varies from culture to culture but seems to be inadequate to achieve population stability. . . . It appears that society must devise something more than the free availability of contraception and abortion. Society at large may have to discourage the raising of children.[7]

These first two recommendations are actually bridging steps to get us from where we are now to where we have to be in order to begin a program of compulsory birth control. Both must be immediately enacted. We no longer have time for years of debate and additional years of gearing up for the task. Yesterday's tomorrow is today; inaction today means tomorrow may be cancelled.

The third plank in a compulsory birth control program is to recognize parenthood as a privilege extended by society, rather than a right inherent in the individual. Accordingly, society has both the right and the duty to limit population when either its physical existence or its quality of life is threatened. Such threats are painfully and increasingly obvious in the United States. There are no rights if there is no society. There is no society if there is no government. It is possible to have government without rights but impossible to have rights without government. Our first task then is to preserve government lest we find ourselves ruled only by the law of the jungle where might makes the only right.

The fourth requirement is for legislation extending the privilege of parenthood to *all* Americans. But no family, regardless of income, education, race, religion or any other consideration shall be entitled to more than two natural children. In the 1940s England adopted a national health insurance program based on four principles: (1) every citizen was to be covered; (2) protection was provided against all major economic and social risks; (3) every citizen was to make the same contribution; and (4) all citizens were to realize the same benefits.[8] These same principles should be applied to America's population policy.

Even though two children per family would not immediately reduce the rate of population growth to zero, it would make it possible to plan urban development and industrial technology on a much firmer basis than is now possible. To advocate only one child per family in order to stabilize population at its present level would arouse the opposition of educators and psychologists concerned about the problems of the "only" child, though there is little to prevent children of different parents from playing and growing up together. The possessive attitude of American parents toward children who are biologically theirs would be difficult to overcome. The desire for a child of each sex is also deeply ingrained, making it extremely difficult for many parents even to consider the prospect of a single child.

Suppose, in 1970, the United States instituted a policy restricting parents to two natural children. By the turn of the twenty-first century, our population would number approximately 245 million. On the other hand, if we continue our present nonpolicy, American population in the year 2000 will number some 300 million. If, for the next three decades, we could devote the money, time and imagination of 55 million people to the problems of slums, environmental pollution, crime, inadequate education, poverty, etc., we would certainly reduce them all. If, on the other hand, all of our efforts must be devoted to satisfying the demands of these same 55 million people for shelter, food, space and purpose, we will have lost all hope for controlling any of these problems. This 55 million is the difference in 30 years between the two-child and the three-child American family. It could be the difference between life and death for this country.

Once we establish the principle of compulsory birth control, the number of children permitted by law can be raised and lowered depending upon social conditions at any given time. Though we set family size at two children now, at some future date it might be necessary to raise or lower permissible family size to accomplish some socially beneficial objective. By varying the number of permitted births every second or third decade or generation, population size could be maintained within predetermined limits. Though the number of permissible births per family might vary between decades or generations, it would not vary within them. For example, the law enacted now could state:

> Public Law Number ——,
> Reversible Fertility Immunization
>
> As of January 1, 1975 it shall be unlawful for any American family to give birth to more than two children. Any family already having two or more natural children on that date shall not be allowed to give birth to another. Toward this end, it is hereby lawfully determined that *all* American citizens above the age of 10 years will, at least one year prior to the aforementioned date present himself/herself for reversible immunization against fertility at a local county health department or physician's office. An official "Certification of Immunization" shall be issued to and in the name of each citizen so treated. Said certification shall be signed by the authorized medical practitioner who administered the immunization and shall be entered into the official records of the county in which immunization occurred. After marriage, any citizen may present himself/herself at a local county health department or physician's office and obtain a fertility restorer. At the birth of the second child, immunity against fertility shall be readministered to both parents. If the first birth shall be multiple, no other births shall be permitted to that mother, and both parents shall thereupon be re-immunized.

By the year 2000, the two-child family will have reached a United States population of approximately 245 million. Social policy at that time may indicate that the number of permissible births per family should be lowered to one for a decade or two. Once the principle of compulsory birth control has been established, it would be easier than at present to convince the public that a family size of only one child might be necessary for a time. Such periodic changes in the allowable number of children would maintain population size at manageable and predictable levels.

The permissible number of births per family could obviously be changed from time to time in response to social need. But under no circumstances would there be more than one permissible maximum in operation at any one time. At any given time, no family would be entitled to more children than all other families. That this could happen is perhaps the most serious objection raised by opponents of compulsory birth control.

Richard Stiller, Associate Director of the Information Center on Population Problems, contends that:

> Compulsion under our present social structures must inevitably degenerate into discrimination. The politically powerful majority would quickly see to it that the fertility of the powerless minority—the poor and the nonwhite—is restricted while theirs is left alone. The rich would then go on doing just as they please, having all the children they can "afford" on the grounds that this is no danger to society. The poor would be forced to have fewer children because they, obviously, cannot "take care" of as many.[9]

This is a point of view which cannot and should not be dismissed lightly. For the rights of the minority must be jealously guarded. I wish that our past performance in protecting minority rights had been more just, less arbitrary. But we cannot change the past, and we dare not deny it, lest all that we say be dismissed as so much claptrap.

But we are not bound by history to repeat our mistakes. It is certainly within our power to devise a population policy which treats all people alike, allowing no special privilege nor imposing any peculiar burden. We *can* do it; we *must* do it.

There is a great deal of evidence appearing to suggest that our nation and the entire world community is much more sensitive to minority rights now than at any time in the past. Minority groups today occupy a position of considerable social and political power. Their support or opposition has significant impact on the eventual disposition of social issues.

In a way, the argument which pits the "politically powerful majority" against the "powerless minority" is an oversimplified and misleading picture of reality. The truth of the matter is that America is a social mosaic composed of thousands of minority groups, the exact number depending upon the issue under consideration. The agreement necessary for action is possible only because some of these groups form short-lived alliances to achieve an end which, for different reasons and in varying degrees, is attractive to each. That the Congress of the United States acts in this way simply reflects the operating principles for the country as a whole.

Suppose we do pass a law restricting family size to two children. What happens if triplets, quads, or quints are born to a family? Or suppose the first birth was a single and the second produces twins or more? What do we do with the children and the parents? There are at least three answers to that question: the science fiction, the punitive and the workable. First the science fiction.

Medical science is now working on a procedure to determine the sex of a child before birth, enabling the parents to find out, shortly after conception, the sex of their unborn child. Other medical procedures are being studied which would allow parents to select the sex of their future child prior to conception. Now if science can develop techniques to predetermine and program the sex of a child, it doesn't require much imagination to think that the number of children can be similarly treated. However I see this as a wholly unrealistic and impractical approach to the question. Certainly science can accomplish this objective if we give it free rein. But there are a few thousand social objectives more demanding of our attention than these medical playthings.

The second answer to our question is to punish excess parenthood. If more than two children are born to a woman, we could take those children from the parents and offer them for adoption and/or fine or imprison the parents. Laws presently governing parenthood provide certain punishments for parents deemed by the courts, for reasons of abuse, neglect or inability, to be unfit. Such laws could be extended to include overly prolific parenthood as a type of unfitness. This approach can be justified, however, only if the parents in question have knowingly avoided or willfully disobeyed the restrictions on parenthood. If, for example, they avoided reversible immunization by deceit or fraud or if they illegally obtained a fertility restorer, then they would be guilty of breaking the law and therefore subject to prosecution as they would be for disobeying any other law. But if they had obeyed the law and still gave birth to more than the permissible number of children, the parents themselves would decide whether to keep the extra children or allow them to be adopted.

The simplest and most workable response to parents who through no fault or intent give birth to more than two children is to do nothing. Most human births are single; multiple births are rare, with each ascending number being rarer than the lower one. If the multiple birth occurred first, the chances are greatest that it would be twins, in which case the completed family size would have been accomplished all at once, and no future births would be allowable. If the second birth were multiple or if the first were triplets or greater, then the permissible family size would have been inadvertently exceeded. No penalties would be attached in this case. These are simply the risks that are run. In any public health program, diseases occur despite our best efforts to control them.

If the United States passed a law which by 1975 restricted families to two children, what about all those families who now have more? What would be done to them? The answer is obvious: nothing. There is a provision in the United States Constitution that laws cannot be applied ex post facto, that is, they cannot be made to declare unlawful, behavior which at the time of its occurrence was legal. An act cannot be undone, and justice does not permit later punishment by a law that did not exist when the act was committed.

The fifth requirement for a compulsory birth control program is the designation of public and private funds sufficient to develop the birth control technology necessary to implement the program. Without vast sums of money and the political support of government, the fertility immunization technology on which this whole program rests will never be available. Ten billion dollars a year must immediately be applied to research and development of this new contraceptive. While to some this may sound like a great deal of money, it represents only five percent of the federal budget. An investment of this magnitude could be expected to realize a savings of approximately 26 to 100 dollars for each dollar invested.[10] Ten billion dollars spent now for contraceptive technology will provide us with at least 260 billion dollars in total economic benefits each year. No one program can promise so much. But if we continue our funding at its present starvation level or even if we increase it by the piddling amounts being mentioned by our more progressive national leaders,[11] we will never achieve the necessary objective.

With adequate funding and political support the necessary contraceptives could be, within the next few years, as available and as pleasant as the sugar cube polio vaccine. Population research, however, will have to get higher priority than it presently does. During Senate hearings on family planning in December 1969, Senator Thomas Eagleton (D-Mo.) compared expenditures by the National Institute of Health: cancer, $185 million; heart disease, $165 million; allergies, $105 million and population, $10.8 million.[12]

In order to generate the necessary public and political support, the program should be given a name other than compulsory birth control. The use of another word, though it would not change the intent or operation of the program, would certainly increase its attractiveness. The Social Security Administration labels the monthly deductions from wages which it compels as FICA—Federal Income Contributory Act—thus giving the program an appearance of voluntarism which, in fact, does not exist. Various Congressional committees in 1969 and 1970 considered introducing legislation for a compulsory health care plan to cover all Americans. In their deliberations, these politically sophisticated individuals described their proposals as "universal," emphasizing the program's coverage, rather than "compulsory" which would focus public attention on methods of enforcement.

I have purposely called my suggested policies and programs "compulsory." To use a less provocative adjective might win a few more friends initially, but it would not attract the necessary attention. We are all like the mule which the farmer bought after having been told that he only had to whisper in the mule's ear to get it to work. After a few futile efforts at whispering in the mule's ear, the farmer sent for its previous owner. Upon his arrival, the prior owner picked up a two-by-four and belted the animal across the head, and then whispered gently in the mule's ear. To the astonished farmer, the first owner explained, "First you have to get his attention."

My task is to get the attention of as many people as possible. Until we are all focused on the problem, we cannot get on with the job that must be done.

The sixth step necessary for control of population growth is the creation of a National Birth Control Administration, whose task it would be to supervise the operation of population programs and to ensure compliance with all regulations. This agency would be patterned after the presently existing National Air Pollution Control Administration and the Environmental Control Administration.

The National Birth Control Administration (NBCA) would

be responsible for establishing federal guidelines for state and local Birth Control offices operating under the authority of the NBCA. It would be their combined task to project population trends, to determine an efficient population size for the United States, and to recommend to the Congress any needed change in allowable family size. The NBCA would also be responsible for the expenditures of public money for contraceptive research and development.

After enactment of the above six proposals designed to control the size and growth rate of the United States, this country must insist that recipients of its foreign aid act accordingly. America could not then be accused, as it is now, of urging other countries to control their population while doing nothing about its own. Latin-American countries are particularly prone to this assessment of our efforts. Many of them see our attempts to institute or encourage their family planning programs as nationalistic aggrandizement. By keeping South American birth rates down, the United States will continue to have more people, and as the traditional dogma would have it, more power. Nothing this country can say will dispel these fears so long as we ask others to do what we are unwilling or unable to do ourselves. Examples speak louder than exhortations.

Some will call these proposals radical, but most of us will live to see them enacted. The question is whether it will be done out of foresight or hindsight. Will our vision of the future and our compassion for people converge to produce a meaningful population policy now, or will we act only in retrospect when, frustrated and afraid, we have passed the point of no return?

But what if America unilaterally declared a moritorium on its internal population growth while other countries continued their reckless breeding habits? Would not this country be weakened and soon overrun by alien hordes? The answer is "No." In fact, we will escape being overrun only if we can bring ourselves to control our population growth. How can that be? Let me explain.

America has been principally responsible throughout history for the development of death control technology. Never did we stop to ask before utilizing such a discovery or invention whether other countries would continue their old dying habits. Because Americans would benefit directly, the technology was applied. As the American death rate went down, other countries began to request help in reducing theirs. These countries were receptive to death control for two reasons: first, because people simply want to live longer; secondly, and perhaps just as important, they could see the beneficial results in this country.

The same process is bound to occur with birth control. If we can reduce our own population growth, thus freeing tremendous resources for use in attacking our multiplicity of social ills; if we can educate, feed, clothe, house and involve our people as all people have a right to expect; if we can discipline ourselves politically and socially, we will not wait long before all nations of the world are seeking our help.

No other nation in the world is as capable as the United States, by virtue of its resources and its political philosophy, of providing the necessary leadership in this area. If our country does not do it, it simply will not be done. And if it is not done, neither our resources nor our political philosophy can survive the impending human tidal wave.

Our only choice is to lead—or to die!

CHAPTER NOTES

1

1. William Paddock and Paul Paddock, *Famine 1975! America's Decision: Who Will Survive?* (Boston: Little, Brown and Co., 1967), Chapter IX.
2. Wayne H. Davis, "Overpopulated America," *The New Republic,* Vol. 162, No. 2, Issue 2872 (January 10, 1970), p. 13.
3. Reprinted from *Psychology Today* Magazine (January 1970). Copyright © Communications (Research) Machines Inc.
4. Conrad Taeuber and Irene B. Taeuber, *The Changing Population of the United States,* The Census Monograph Series (New York: John Wiley and Sons, Inc., 1948), Chapter I.
5. These figures represent the author's own calculations based on information taken from a variety of sources, such as *The World Almanac* and various governmental publications.
6. Sociologist Philip M. Hauser has said that at our standard of living, the world's total products could support half a billion people. See Durward L. Allen, "Population, Resources and the Great Complexity," PRB Selection No. 29 (Washington, D.C.: Population Reference Bureau, Inc., 1969), p. 4.
7. According to government estimates the per capita production of refuse in the U.S. rose from 2.75 lbs. per day in 1920 to 4.5 lbs. per day in 1965 and is now increasing at the rate of 4% per year.
8. Donald E. Carr, "Only the Giant Car-eater Can Save Us," *The New York Times Magazine* (May 4, 1969), p. 87. © 1969 by The New York Times Company. Reprinted by permission.
9. See *Needed: Clean Air* (Greenfield, Mass.: Channing L. Bete Co.,

Inc. 1969), p. 8 and *Air Pollution Primer* (New York: National Tuberculosis and Respiratory Disease Association, 1969), p. 71.

10. *Air Pollution Primer,* p. 71.

11. *Ibid.*

12. *Ibid.,* p. 70.

13. *Needed: Clean Air,* p. 8.

14. C. B. Luce, "America the Dirty," *McCalls,* Vol. 192 (July 1965), p. 28; see also Howard Lewis, *With Every Breath You Take* (New York: Crown Publishers, 1965).

15. K. L. Johnson and others, "Carbon Monoxide and Air Pollution from Automobile Emissions in New York City," *Science,* Vol. 160 (April 5, 1968), pp. 67–68. Copyright 1968 by the American Association for the Advancement of Science.

16. *Air Pollution Primer,* p. 19.

17. *Ibid.,* p. 83.

18. Theodore Berland, "Our Dirty Sky," *Today's Health,* published by the American Medical Association, XLIV (March 1966), pp. 40–45.

19. *Ibid.*

20. "Cities Draft Stricter Control Curbs," *Public Management,* XXXII (August 1950), p. 179.

21. *Air Pollution Primer,* p. 60.

22. Berland, pp. 40–45.

23. *Air Pollution Primer.*

24. "Watery Grave for Lake Michigan? Result of Industrial Waste," *Business Week* (October 21, 1967), pp. 103–104.

25. Howard Earl, "That Dirty Mess: Water Pollution," *Today's Health,* published by the American Medical Association, XLIV (March 1966), pp. 52–56.

26. Stewart Udall, "Physical Environment: If We Don't Control It, It May Control Us," *Nation's Business,* LVI (June 1968), pp. 64–66.

27. J. Walsh, "Pollution: The Wake of the Torrey Canyon," *Science,* Vol. 160 (April 12, 1968), pp. 167–169. Copyright 1968 by the American Association for the Advancement of Science.

28. Anthony Bailey, "Noise Is a Slow Agent of Death," *The New York Times Magazine* (Nov. 23, 1969): "Assault on the Ear," *Newsweek,* LXVII, No. 70 (April 4, 1966), pp. 70–71.

29. Anthony Bailey, "Noise Is a Slow Agent of Death," *The New York Times Magazine* (November 23, 1969). © 1969 by The New York Times Company. Reprinted by permission.

30. Victor Block, "Where Has All Our Silence Gone," *This Week* (August 10, 1969), pp. 4–5.

31. "When Noise Annoys—Time Essay," *Time,* LXXXVIII, No. 24 & 25 (August 19, 1966), pp. 24–25.

32. "Assault on the Ear," *Newsweek,* LXVII, No. 70 (April 4, 1966), p. 71.

33. "One Man's Trash," *Scientific American* (May 1966), p. 52.

34. Wilson G. Smillie, *Public Health Administration in the United States* (New York: The Macmillan Co., 1940), p. 11.

35. Joan Jensen, "Overpopulation: A Social Conservation Crisis," *Childbirth Education,* II, No. 2 & 3 (Spring-Summer 1969), p. 6.

2

1. George Wald, "A Generation in Search of a Future," *The New Yorker* (March 22, 1969), pp. 29–31.

2. Harold Rosenberg, from "Death in the Wilderness," quoted by Morris Dickstein in "Allen Ginsberg and the 60's," *Commentary* (January 1970), p. 64. Reprinted from *Commentary,* by permission; Copyright © 1970 by the American Jewish Committee.

3. J. Abner Peddiwell, *The Saber-Tooth Curriculum* (New York: McGraw-Hill Book Co., Inc., 1939).

4. C. P. Snow, "What Is the World's Greatest Need?" *The New York Times Magazine* (April 2, 1961), p. 7. © 1961 by The New York Times Company. Reprinted by permission.

3

1. Hugh Moore Fund (newspaper advertisement).
2. Marston Bates, *The Prevalence of People* (New York: Charles Scribner's Sons, 1955), p. 27.
3. "1969 World Population Data Sheet" (Washington, D.C.: Population Reference Bureau, 1969).
4. *The Kansas City Times* (December 1, 1969).
5. From *People! Challenge to Survival* by William Vogt. Published by William Sloane Associates, Inc. Reprinted by permission of William Morrow and Company, Inc. Copyright © 1960 by William Vogt.
6. "The Most Polluted City," *Newsweek* (November 3, 1969), p. 67.
7. Paul Ehrlich, *The Population Bomb* (New York: Ballantine Books, Inc., 1968), p. 87.
8. Louis Wirth, "Urbanism as a Way of Life," *American Journal of Sociology,* XLIV (July 1938), pp. 1–24.
9. George Gallup, "Many Americans Dream of Escaping the Big City Pace," *The Kansas City Star* (February 19, 1970), Sec. A, p. 1.
10. All crime information cited in this discussion is based upon the *Uniform Crime Reports* compiled by the F.B.I. and published by the U.S. Department of Justice.
11. William Denver, "Problems of Law Enforcement in the Large Cities of the United States," *American Bar Association Journal,* XIII, No. 8 (August 1926), p. 554.
12. *The Kansas City Star* (March 1, 1970).
13. David Riesman with Nathan Glazer and Reuel Denny, *The Lonely Crowd, A Study of the Changing American Character* (Garden City, N.Y.: Doubleday and Co., Inc., 1950).
14. James H. S. Bossard, "The Law of Family Interaction," *American Journal of Sociology,* L (1945), pp. 292–294. Also, "A Spatial Index for Family Interaction," *American Sociological Review,* XVI (1951), pp. 243–246.

15. Desmond Morris, *The Human Zoo* (New York: McGraw-Hill Book Co., Inc., 1969).

16. From, "Population Density and Social Pathology," by John B. Calhoun. Copyright © 1962 by Scientific American, Inc. All rights reserved. Reprinted by permission.

17. *Ibid.*

18. Durward L. Allen, "Population, Resources and the Great Complexity," PRB Selection No. 29 (Washington, D.C.: Population Reference Bureau, Inc., 1969), p. 4.

4

1. Margaret Mead, "The Crisis of Our Overcrowded World," *Redbook Magazine* (October 1969), p. 42.

2. *The Determinants and Consequences of Population Trends* (New York: The United Nations, 1953), Chapter III; reprinted in Joseph J. Spengler and Otis Duncan, eds., *Population Theories and Policies* (Glencoe, Ill.: The Free Press, 1956).

3. *The Determinants and Consequences of Population Trends,* p. 22.

4. *Ibid.*

5. *Ibid.*

6. *Ibid.,* p. 23.

7. *Ibid.*

8. *Ibid.*

9. *Ibid.,* p. 24.

10. See *The Determinants and Consequences of Population Trends,* pp. 24–25 for an excellent summary of mercantilism.

11. *Ibid.* See also Thomas Malthus, "An Essay on the Principle of Population" (1798). Malthus revised and shortened his 1798 Essay. His 1830 version can be found in *Three Essays on Population* (New York: The New American Library, 1960), pp. 13–59.

12. Herbert Spencer, *The Principles of Biology* (New York: Appleton Company, 1880).

13. Sidney H. Coontz, *Population Theories and the Economic Interpretation* (London: Routledge and Kegan Paul Ltd., 1957), p. 53.

14. *Ibid.*, p. 54.

15. *Ibid.*, p. 55; Spencer, pp. 506–507.

16. *The Determinants and Consequences of Population Trends,* p. 27.

17. *Ibid.*, p. 33.

18. *Ibid.*, p. 34.

19. *Ibid.*, p. 36.

20. *Ibid.*, pp. 39–40.

21. *Ibid.*, p. 40, *Leerboek der Staathuishondkunde.*

22. *The Determinants and Consequences of Population Trends,* p. 41.

23. *Ibid.* See also N. E. Himes, *Medical History of Contraception* (Baltimore, Md.: Williams and Wilkins, 1936).

24. Quoted in Spengler and Duncan, *op. cit.*, p. 28.

25. Warren L. Thompson, "Population," *American Journal of Sociology,* XXXIX (1929), pp. 406–407.

26. C. P. Blacker, "Stages in Population Growth," *Eugenics Review,* XXXIX (1947), pp. 88–102.

27. William Petersen, *Population* (New York: The Macmillan Co., 1961), p. 311.

28. *Ibid.*, p. 492.

29. Frank Lorimer and others, *Culture and Human Fertility* (Paris: UNESCO, 1954).

30. Donald Cowgill, "The Theory of Population Growth Cycles," *American Journal of Sociology,* LV (1949–1950), pp. 163–170.

31. Warren Thompson, *Population Problems* (New York: McGraw-Hill Book Co., Inc., 1942), p. 42.

32. Garrett Hardin, "The Tragedy of the Commons," *Science,* Vol. 162, No. 3859 (December 13, 1968), p. 1243. Copyright 1968 by the American Association for the Advancement of Science.

33. Joan Jensen, "Overpopulation: A Social Conservation Crisis," *Childbirth Education,* II, No. 2 & 3 (Spring-Summer 1969), p. 6.

34. George Lundberg, *Can Science Save Us?* (New York: David McKay Co., Inc., 1941).

35. Robert Oppenheimer as quoted by Robert Jay Lifton, "Absurdity and Common Sense," August 30, 1969, *Saturday Review*, p. 20.

36. Arnold Toynbee, "Why and How I Work," *Saturday Review* (April 5, 1969), p. 24. From *Experiences*. © 1969 by Oxford University. Reprinted by permission.

37. Hardin, *op. cit.*

38. Paul Ehrlich, *The Population Bomb* (New York: Ballantine Books, Inc., 1968), p. 11.

5

1. Senate Bill 2108 (May 8, 1969).

2. Margaret Sanger, in S. Hanan, *Nation*, Vol. 138 (January 31, 1934), pp. 129–130.

3. Morris Udall, "Standing Room Only on Spaceship Earth," *Reader's Digest* (December 1969), p. 134; from *Arizona Republic* (July 27, 1969). Reprinted by permission.

4. Richard D. Lamm, "The Reproductive Revolution," *American Bar Association Journal*, LVI (January 1970), p. 44.

5. N. Lewis and M. Reinhold, *Roman Civilization* (New York: Columbia University Press, 1951), I.

6. K. S. LaTourette, *The Chinese: Their History and Culture*, 3rd ed. rev. (New York: The Macmillan Co., 1946).

7. Kingsley Davis in *Poverty in America*, M. E. Gordon, ed. (San Francisco: Chandler, 1965), pp. 229–319; Lee Rainwater, *And the Poor Get Children* (Chicago: Quandrangle, 1960); A. A. Campbell, "The Role of Family Planning in the Reduction of Poverty," *Journal of Marriage and Family*, XXX (May 1968), pp. 236–245.

8. E. James Lieberman, "Preventive Psychiatry and Family Planning," *Journal of Marriage and Family*, XXVI (November 1964), pp. 471–477.

9. Garrett Hardin, *Planned Parenthood News*, I, No. 2 (May 1969), p. 3.

10. J. M. Murtagh and Sara Harris, *Who Lives in Shadow* (New York: McGraw-Hill Book Co., Inc., 1959), p. 36.

11. H. Brandom, "A Talk with Walter Lippmann at 80 about This Minor Dark Age," *The New York Times Magazine* (September 14, 1969), p. 140. © 1969 by the New York Times Company. Reprinted by permission.

12. L. Miller, "Toward a World of Wanted Children," *Reader's Digest,* XCI (October 1967), p. 89.

13. The Victor Fund for the International Planned Parenthood Federation, No. 8 (Spring 1969), p. 3.

14. Congressional Record, Proceedings and Debate of the 91st Congress, First Session.

15. Planned Parenthood-World Population, "When More Is Less."

16. Alan F. Guttmacher, "Family Planning, The Needs and the Methods," *American Journal of Nursing,* LXIX (June 1969), p. 1230.

17. D. Dempsey, "Dr. Guttmacher Is the Evangelist of Birth Control," *The New York Times Magazine* (February 9, 1969), p. 82; © 1969 by The New York Times Company. Reprinted by permission.

18. *Gallup Poll Research Text* (April 1966), p. 17.

19. From speech by Alice Taylor Day, May 7, 1965 at Planned Parenthood meeting, Milwaukee, Wisconsin.

20. Committee on Population, National Academy of Science-National Research Council Publication No. 1279, p. 6.

21. Richard Day, "Society's Stake in Responsible Parenthood," *American Journal of the Diseases of Childhood,* Vol. 113 (May 1967), pp. 519–521.

22. See Judith Blake, "Population Policy for Americans: Is the Government Being Misled?" *Science,* Vol. 164, No. 3879 (May 2, 1969), pp. 522–529. Copyright 1969 by the American Association for the Advancement of Science.

23. Harriet Pilpel and Nancy Wechsler, "Birth Control, Teenagers and the Law," *Family Planning Perspectives,* I, No. 1 (Spring 1969), p. 29.

24. Kingsley Davis, "Population Policy: Will Current Programs Succeed?" *Science,* Vol. 158 (November 10, 1967), p. 732. Copyright

1967 by the American Association for the Advancement of Science.

25. Russell Lynes, *The Taste Makers* (New York: Houghton-Mifflin Co., 1958).

26. John Galbraith, *The Affluent Society* (Boston: Houghton-Mifflin Co., 1958).

27. "The 'Talk-No Do' Syndrome," *Population Bulletin,* XXV, No. 6 (December 1969), p. 119.

28. Testimony of Alan Guttmacher, M.D., President, Planned Parenthood-World Population, before Senate Committee on Labor and Public Welfare on S.2108, December 8, 1969.

29. *Statistical Abstract of the United States,* 90th Annual Ed. (1969), p. 731.

30. *Population Bulletin, op. cit.,* p. 1.

31. Davis, "Population Policy: Will Current Programs Succeed?" *op. cit.*

32. "The 'Talk-No Do' Syndrome," *op. cit.,* p. 124.

33. *Ibid.,* pp. 125–126.

34 Blake, *op. cit.,* p. 528.

35. The total of 4,739 patients served by Planned Parenthood in 1969 referred to on page 92, includes 2,603 former patients and 2,136 new ones.

36. Alan Guttmacher, "Family Planning, The Needs and the Methods," *op. cit.,* pp. 1229–1234.

37. Passed September 30, 1969; for information contact Zero Population Growth, Inc., 330 Second Street, Los Altos, California 94022.

6

1. Arthur Fink, C. Wilson Anderson and Merril B. Conover, *The Field of Social Work,* 5th ed. (New York: Holt, Rinehart and Winston, Inc., 1968), p. 28.

2. *The New York Times* (April 5, 1935), p. 25.

3. *The New York Times* (May 1, 1936), p. 23.

4. *The New York Times* (April 24, 1937), p. 18.

5. Wilson G. Smillie, *Public Health Administration in the United States* (New York: The Macmillan Co., 1940).

6. *Ibid.,* p. 18.

7. *The Dan Smoot Report,* X, No. 49 (Dec. 7, 1964), p. 391, Dallas, Texas.

8. *Corpus Juris Secundum* (West Publishing Co., 1950), p. 692.

9. Gordon V. Drake, *Sex Education in the Schools* (Tulsa, Oklahoma: Christian Crusade Publications, 1968), p. 28.

10. *Time,* XC (September 22, 1967), p. 86. Reprinted by permission from TIME, The Weekly Newsmagazine; Copyright Time Inc. 1967.

11. Smillie, p. 122.

12. Eric Fromm, *Escape from Freedom* (New York: Farrar & Rinehart, Inc., 1941).

13. Smillie, p. 118.

14. *Corpus Juris Secundum,* XVI A, pp. 213–214.

15. *Ibid.,* LXVII, p. 633.

16. Howard Becker and Harry Elmer Barnes, *Social Thought from Lore to Science* (New York: Dover Publications, Inc., 1961), p. 21.

17. Charles I. Schottland, *The Social Security Program in the United States* (New York: Appleton-Century-Croft, 1963), p. 15.

18. *Ibid.,* p. 24.

19. *Ibid.,* p. 25.

20. *Ibid,* p. 38.

21. Richard Lamm, "The Reproductive Revolution," *American Bar Association Journal,* LVI (January 1970), p. 44.

22. Edward J. Van Allen, *The Trouble With Social Security* (New York: Omnipress, 1969), pp. 17–19.

23. Durward L. Allen, "Population, Resources and the Great Com-

plexity," *Population Reference Bureau,* Selection No. 29 (August 1969), p. 5.

24. Louis Henkin, "Changing Law for the Changing Seas" in *Uses of the Seas,* Edmund A. Gullion, ed. (Englewood Cliffs, N.J.: Prentice-Hall, Inc., 1968), p. 69.

25. "Eminent Domain," *Encyclopaedia Britannica,* VIII, p. 335.

26. *Ibid.*

27. Richard Stiller, "Compulsory Birth Control: Yes or No," *Sexology,* XXXVI, No. 9 (April 1970), pp. 30–34.

7

1. Thomas Eisner and others, "Population Control, Sterilization, and Ignorance," *Science,* Vol. 167, no. 3917 (January 23, 1970), p. 337. Copyright 1970 by the American Association for the Advancement of Science.

2. *Statistical Abstract of the United States,* U.S. Bureau of the Census, Washington, D.C.: see both the 89th ed. (1968) and the 90th ed. (1969).

3. Carl T. Rowan, "Blacks Being Misled on Birth Control," *Kansas City Star* (February 2, 1970).

4. *Ibid.*

5. Ralph Z. Hallow, "Blacks Cry Genocide," *Nation,* Vol. 208 (April 28, 1969), p. 537.

6. See the transcript of testimony on Senate Bill 2108 before the Health Subcommittee of the Senate Committee on Labor and Public Welfare, December 8–9, 1969; see also Richard Lincoln, "S.2108: Capitol Hill Debates the Future of Population and Family Planning," *Family Planning Perspectives,* II, No. 1 (January 1970), p. 12.

7. Hallow, p. 536.

8. Ronald Freedman and others, "Socio-Economic Factors in Religious Differentials in Marriage," *American Sociological Review,* XXVI (August 1961), pp. 608–614.

9. "The 'Talk-NoDo' Syndrome", *Population Bulletin,* XXV, No. 6 (December 1969), p. 124.

10. Michael Harrington, *The Other America* (New York: The Macmillan Co., 1962).

11. Rousas J. Rushdoony, *The Myth of Overpopulation* (Nutley, N.J.: The Craig Press, 1969), p. 8.

12. Frank S. Mead, *Handbook of Denominations in the United States* (Nashville, Tenn.: Abingdon Press, 1951).

13. Earl J. Reeves, "The Population Explosion and Christian Concern," in *Protest and Politics,* Robert Clouse and others, eds. (Greenwood, S.C.: The Attic Press Co., Inc., 1968), p. 190.

14. Arthur Matthews, "Birth Control: Which Methods Are Moral?" *Christianity Today,* XI (February 17, 1967), p. 43.

15. Elizabeth Draper, *Birth Control in the Modern World* (Baltimore, Md.: Penguin Books, Inc., 1965), p. 154.

16. Margaret Sanger, *My Fight for Birth Control* (New York: Farrar & Rinehart, 1935).

17. "Commission on Rhythm," *The Linacre Quarterly Review* (February 1966), pp. 1–6.

18. *Ibid.*

19. Draper, *op. cit.,* p. 153.

20. *Ibid.,* p. 154.

21. Pascal K. Whelpton, Arthur A. Campbell and John E. Patterson, *Fertility and Family Planning in the United States* (Princeton, N.J.: Princeton University Press, 1966), p. 178.

22. *Ibid.,* p. 27.

23. *Ibid,* p. 38.

24. *Ibid.,* pp. 36–37.

25. *Ibid.,* p. 40.

26. Morris L. Ernst and Alan U. Schwartz, *Censorship: The Search for the Obscene* (New York: The Macmillan Co., 1964), p. 31. Copyright © Joan E. Goldstein and Alan U. Schwartz 1964.

27. *Ibid.,* pp. 31–32.

28. Thomas Eisner and others, *op. cit.*

8

1. Editorial, *The New York Times* (July 6, 1969).
2. See Isabel C. Milton, "Contraceptive Practices Past and Present," *The Canadian Nurse* (October 1967), pp. 29–31; Elizabeth Draper, *Birth Control in the Modern World* (Baltimore, Md.: Penguin Books, Inc., 1965), Chapter IV; N. E. Himes, *Medical History of Contraception* (Baltimore, Md.: Williams and Wilkins, 1936).
3. John Noonan, *Contraception* (Cambridge, Mass.: Harvard University Press, 1966), p. 9.
4. Draper, p. 75.
5. *Ibid.*, pp. 77–78.
6. *Ibid.*, p. 57; Milton, p. 31.
7. Draper, p. 57.
8. "The Physician and Contraceptive Sterilization" (New York: The Association for Voluntary Sterilization, 1969), p. 3.
9. *Ibid.*, p. 1.
10. *Ibid.*, p. 3.
11. P. Kerby, "Abortion: Laws and Attitudes," *Nation,* Vol. 204 (June 12, 1967), pp. 754–756.
12. *Ibid.*
13. *Ibid.*
14. "The Desperate Dilemmas of Abortion," *Time,* XC (October 13, 1967), pp. 32–33.
15. "The Drug That Left a Trail of Heartbreak," *Life,* LIII (August 10, 1962), pp. 24–36.
16. Albert Q. Maisel, "The Growing Battle over Abortion Reform," *Reader's Digest,* XCIV (June 1969), pp. 152–158.
17. Draper, p. 80.
18. Alan F. Guttmacher, *The Complete Book of Birth Control* (New York: Ballantine Books, 1961), p. 39.

19. For an excellent medical discussion of IUD's see J. Robert Wilson, M.D., "Intrauterine Contraceptive Devices: Practical Considerations in Their Uses," in Alan Rubin, M.D., ed., *Family Planning Today* (Philadelphia: F. A. Davis Co., 1969), Chapter V.

20. "Verdict on IUD's," *Newsweek* (January 29, 1968), p. 56.

21. Draper, pp. 56–66; Milton, p. 31.

22. See Joseph W. Goldzieher, M.D., "Oral Contraceptives: Which One and For Whom?" in Rubin, Chapter IV.

23. See Louis M. Hellman, M.D., "Oral Contraceptives: Safety and Complications," in Rubin, Chapter III; Francis J. Kane, Jr., M.D., "Psychiatric Reactions to Oral Contraceptives," *American Journal of Obstetrics and Gynecology* (December 1, 1968), pp. 1053–1063.

24. Alan F. Guttmacher, "Family Planning, The Needs and the Methods," *American Journal of Nursing,* LXIX, No. 6 (June 1969), p. 1232.

25. "The Gallup Poll." Copyright 1970 by The American Institute of Public Opinion. Used by permission.

26. For the longer warning, see *Rodale's Environment Action Bulletin,* VIII, No. 19 (St. Emmaus, Pa.: May 9, 1970).

27. One recent book on the pill, poorly documented but highly critical is Harold Williams, M.D., *Pregnant or Dead?* (San Francisco: New Perspective Publications, 1969).

28. Guttmacher, "Family Planning, The Needs and the Methods," *op. cit.*

29. From J. F. Hulka, "A Mathematical Model Study of Contraceptive Efficiency and Unplanned Pregnancies," *American Journal of Obstetrics and Gynecology,* Vol. 104 (1969), pp. 443–447.

30. *Ibid.*, p. 443.

31. See Sheldon J. Segal, "What Will the Future Bring in Family Planning?" in Rubin, *op. cit.*, Chapter X; Alan F. Guttmacher, "Family Planning, The Needs and the Methods, *op. cit.*, pp. 1229–1234.

32. "Safe Substitute for the Pill," *Science Digest,* LXVI (August 1969), p. 60.

33. Alan F. Guttmacher, *Babies by Choice or by Chance* (Garden City, N.Y.: Copyright Doubleday and Company, Inc., 1959).

34. Carl Djerassi, "Prognosis for the Development of New Chemical Birth-Control Agents," *Science*, Vol. 166 (October 24, 1969), pp. 468–473. Copyright 1969 by the American Association for the Advancement of Science.

35. *Ibid.*, p. 472.

36. Richard Lincoln, "S.2108: Capitol Hill Debates the Future of Population and Family Planning," *Family Planning Perspectives,* II, No. 1 (January 1970), pp. 6–12.

9

1. Vance Packard, *The Sexual Wilderness* (New York: David McKay Co., Inc., 1968).

2. Howard Becker and Harry Elmer Barnes, *Social Thought from Lore to Science,* 3rd ed. (New York: Dover Publications, Inc., 1961), I, p. 238.

3. William H. Leach, ed., *The Cokesbury Marriage Manual* (New York: Abingdon-Cokesbury Press, 1945), pp. 147–149.

4. Margaret Sanger, *My Fight for Birth Control* (New York: Farrar & Rinehart, 1935).

5. *Three Essays on Population,* Thomas Malthus, Julian Huxley, Frederick Osborn (New York: The New American Library, 1960), p. 111.

10

1. Richard Day, "Society's Stake in Responsible Parenthood," *American Journal of the Diseases of Childhood,* Vol. 113 (May 1967), pp. 519–521.

2. Thomas Freijka, "Reflections on the Demographic Conditions Needed to Establish a U.S. Stationary Population Growth," *Population Studies,* XXII (November 1969), pp. 379–397.

3. Day, p. 520.

4. Freijka, p. 384.

5. Day, p. 520.

6. Freijka, p. 382.

7. Richard D. Lamm, "The Reproductive Revolution," *American Bar Association Journal,* LVI (January 1970), p. 44.

8. Arthur E. Fink, C. Wilson Anderson and Merrill B. Conover, *The Field of Social Work,* 5th ed. (New York: Holt, Rinehart and Winston, Inc., 1968), p. 30.

9. Richard Stiller, "Compulsory Birth Control. Yes or No?" *Sexology,* XXXVI, No. 9 (April 1970), p. 31.

10. Arthur A. Campbell, "The Role of Family Planning in the Reduction of Poverty," *Journal of Marriage and Family* (May 1968), p. 326; Stephen Enke, "Birth Control for Economic Development," *Science,* Vol. 164, No. 3881 (May 16, 1969), p. 798. Copyright 1969 by the American Association for the Advancement of Science. Campbell estimates that each dollar spent for contraception will produce $26 in economic benefits. Enke says that money spent for birth control can be 100 times more effective in raising per capita output than more traditional economic investments.

11. The bill introduced by Senator Joseph Tydings (May 1969) "would authorize $35 million in fiscal year 1971 to expand our program of population-related biomedical and social science research . . . $12 million would be made available for the construction of population research centers in universities and medical schools."

12. Richard Lincoln, "S.2108: Capitol Hill Debates the Future of Population and Family Planning," *Family Planning Perspectives,* II, No. 1 (January 1970), p. 10.